50 Premium Chinese Restaurant Recipes for Home

By: Kelly Johnson

Table of Contents

- Peking Duck
- General Tso's Chicken
- Kung Pao Chicken
- Sweet and Sour Pork
- Mongolian Beef
- Lemon Chicken
- Beef and Broccoli
- Orange Chicken
- Szechuan Shrimp
- Mapo Tofu
- Hot and Sour Soup
- Wonton Soup
- Egg Drop Soup
- Fried Rice
- Lo Mein
- Chow Mein
- Dumplings
- Spring Rolls
- Crab Rangoon
- Char Siu (BBQ Pork)
- Ma Po Tofu
- Mongolian Beef
- Sichuan Spicy Noodles
- Beef with Black Bean Sauce
- Lemon Shrimp
- Thai Basil Chicken
- Crispy Honey Garlic Chicken
- Sweet and Sour Chicken
- Dim Sum
- Shanghai Soup Dumplings
- Hot Pot
- Teriyaki Chicken

- Shrimp with Lobster Sauce
- Chinese BBQ Ribs
- Prawn and Chive Dumplings
- Salt and Pepper Squid
- Chinese Broccoli with Oyster Sauce
- Beef Chow Fun
- Egg Foo Young
- Crab Fried Rice
- Cantonese Roast Pork
- Sichuan Cold Noodles
- Black Pepper Beef
- Chinese Chicken Salad
- Tofu and Vegetable Stir-Fry
- Honey Walnut Shrimp
- Szechuan Eggplant
- Steamed Fish with Ginger and Scallions
- Chinese Scallion Pancakes
- Lotus Leaf Wrapped Chicken

Peking Duck

Ingredients:

- **For the Duck:**
    - 1 whole duck (about 5-6 lbs or 2.3-2.7 kg)
    - 1 tablespoon salt
    - 1 tablespoon sugar
    - 1 tablespoon soy sauce
    - 1 tablespoon rice vinegar
    - 1 tablespoon honey
    - 2 cups water
- **For the Glaze:**
    - 1/4 cup honey
    - 2 tablespoons soy sauce
    - 2 tablespoons rice vinegar
    - 1 tablespoon hoisin sauce
    - 1 tablespoon sesame oil
- **For Serving:**
    - Chinese pancakes or tortillas
    - Hoisin sauce
    - Thinly sliced scallions
    - Cucumber (julienned)
    - Additional hoisin sauce for dipping

Instructions:

1. **Prepare the Duck:**
    - Clean the duck thoroughly and remove any excess fat. Pat it dry with paper towels.
    - Rub the duck inside and out with salt and sugar. Place it on a rack over a tray and refrigerate, uncovered, for at least 4 hours or overnight to allow the skin to dry out.
2. **Blanch the Duck:**
    - Preheat your oven to 375°F (190°C).
    - In a large pot, bring 2 cups of water to a boil. Carefully lower the duck into the boiling water for 1-2 minutes to blanch the skin. Remove the duck and let it drain and cool for a few minutes.
3. **Prepare the Glaze:**
    - In a small saucepan, combine honey, soy sauce, rice vinegar, hoisin sauce, and sesame oil. Heat over medium heat until the mixture is well combined and slightly thickened. Set aside.
4. **Roast the Duck:**

- Brush the duck all over with the glaze mixture.
- Place the duck on a rack in a roasting pan. Roast in the preheated oven for about 1 1/2 to 2 hours, or until the skin is crispy and golden brown. Baste the duck with the glaze every 30 minutes.
- For extra crispiness, you can also increase the oven temperature to 400°F (200°C) during the last 10-15 minutes of roasting.

5. **Serve:**
    - Let the duck rest for 10 minutes before carving.
    - To serve, thinly slice the duck into pieces. Serve with Chinese pancakes, hoisin sauce, sliced scallions, and julienned cucumber.

Enjoy your homemade Peking Duck!

General Tso's Chicken

Ingredients:

- **For the Chicken:**
    - 1 lb (450g) boneless, skinless chicken thighs (cut into bite-sized pieces)
    - 1 cup all-purpose flour
    - 1/2 cup cornstarch
    - 1 teaspoon baking powder
    - 1/2 teaspoon salt
    - 1/2 teaspoon ground black pepper
    - 1/2 cup water (or as needed to make a batter)
    - Vegetable oil (for frying)
- **For the Sauce:**
    - 1/2 cup chicken broth
    - 1/4 cup soy sauce
    - 1/4 cup rice vinegar
    - 1/4 cup hoisin sauce
    - 2 tablespoons sugar
    - 1 tablespoon cornstarch mixed with 2 tablespoons water (cornstarch slurry)
    - 2 tablespoons vegetable oil
    - 3-4 cloves garlic (minced)
    - 1 tablespoon fresh ginger (minced)
    - 2-3 dried red chilies (or to taste, optional for heat)
    - 1 tablespoon sesame oil
- **For Garnish:**
    - Sliced green onions
    - Sesame seeds (optional)

Instructions:

1. **Prepare the Chicken:**
    - In a large bowl, combine flour, cornstarch, baking powder, salt, and pepper.
    - Gradually add water to the dry ingredients, stirring until you have a thick batter. Coat the chicken pieces in the batter.
    - Heat vegetable oil in a large skillet or wok over medium-high heat. Fry the chicken pieces in batches until golden brown and crispy, about 4-5 minutes per batch. Remove the chicken and drain on paper towels.
2. **Prepare the Sauce:**
    - In a small bowl, mix together chicken broth, soy sauce, rice vinegar, hoisin sauce, and sugar. Set aside.
    - In the same skillet or wok, heat 2 tablespoons vegetable oil over medium heat. Add minced garlic, ginger, and dried red chilies (if using). Sauté for 1-2 minutes until fragrant.

- Pour in the sauce mixture and bring to a simmer. Stir in the cornstarch slurry to thicken the sauce. Cook for 1-2 minutes until the sauce has thickened.
3. **Combine Chicken and Sauce:**
    - Add the fried chicken pieces to the sauce and toss to coat evenly. Stir in sesame oil for extra flavor.
4. **Serve:**
    - Transfer the General Tso's Chicken to a serving dish. Garnish with sliced green onions and sesame seeds if desired.
    - Serve with steamed rice or noodles.

Enjoy your flavorful and crispy General Tso's Chicken!

Kung Pao Chicken

Ingredients:

- **For the Marinade:**
    - 1 lb (450g) boneless, skinless chicken thighs or breasts (cut into bite-sized pieces)
    - 1 tablespoon soy sauce
    - 1 tablespoon rice wine or dry sherry
    - 1 tablespoon cornstarch
- **For the Sauce:**
    - 1/4 cup soy sauce
    - 2 tablespoons rice vinegar
    - 2 tablespoons hoisin sauce
    - 2 tablespoons sugar
    - 1 tablespoon cornstarch mixed with 2 tablespoons water (cornstarch slurry)
    - 1/2 cup water or chicken broth
- **For Stir-Frying:**
    - 2 tablespoons vegetable oil
    - 4-6 dried red chilies (or to taste)
    - 1 tablespoon Sichuan peppercorns (optional, for a numbing heat)
    - 1 bell pepper (red or green, chopped)
    - 1 medium onion (chopped)
    - 3 cloves garlic (minced)
    - 1 tablespoon fresh ginger (minced)
    - 1/2 cup roasted peanuts (or cashews)
- **For Garnish:**
    - Sliced green onions
    - Fresh cilantro (optional)

Instructions:

1. **Marinate the Chicken:**
    - In a bowl, combine chicken pieces with soy sauce, rice wine or sherry, and cornstarch. Mix well and let it marinate for at least 15 minutes.
2. **Prepare the Sauce:**
    - In a separate bowl, mix together soy sauce, rice vinegar, hoisin sauce, sugar, cornstarch slurry, and water or chicken broth. Set aside.
3. **Stir-Fry the Chicken:**
    - Heat vegetable oil in a large skillet or wok over medium-high heat.
    - Add dried red chilies and Sichuan peppercorns (if using). Stir-fry for about 30 seconds until fragrant, being careful not to burn them.

- Add the marinated chicken to the skillet. Stir-fry until the chicken is cooked through and slightly browned, about 5-7 minutes. Remove the chicken from the skillet and set aside.
4. **Stir-Fry Vegetables:**
    - In the same skillet, add a bit more oil if needed. Add bell pepper and onion, and stir-fry for 2-3 minutes until they start to soften.
    - Add minced garlic and ginger, and stir-fry for another 1-2 minutes.
5. **Combine Chicken and Sauce:**
    - Return the cooked chicken to the skillet. Pour in the prepared sauce and stir to coat everything evenly.
    - Cook for an additional 2-3 minutes, until the sauce has thickened and everything is well combined.
    - Stir in roasted peanuts.
6. **Serve:**
    - Transfer the Kung Pao Chicken to a serving dish. Garnish with sliced green onions and fresh cilantro if desired.
    - Serve hot with steamed rice or noodles.

Enjoy your flavorful and spicy Kung Pao Chicken!

Sweet and Sour Pork

Ingredients:

- **For the Pork:**
    - 1 lb (450g) boneless pork loin or pork shoulder (cut into bite-sized cubes)
    - 1/2 cup all-purpose flour
    - 1/4 cup cornstarch
    - 1/2 teaspoon salt
    - 1/2 teaspoon ground black pepper
    - 1 egg
    - 1/2 cup cold water
    - Vegetable oil (for frying)
- **For the Sauce:**
    - 1/2 cup ketchup
    - 1/2 cup rice vinegar
    - 1/4 cup soy sauce
    - 1/4 cup sugar
    - 1/2 cup pineapple juice
    - 2 tablespoons cornstarch mixed with 2 tablespoons water (cornstarch slurry)
- **For the Stir-Fry:**
    - 2 tablespoons vegetable oil
    - 1 red bell pepper (cut into chunks)
    - 1 green bell pepper (cut into chunks)
    - 1 onion (cut into chunks)
    - 1 cup pineapple chunks (canned or fresh)
    - 3 cloves garlic (minced)
    - 1 tablespoon fresh ginger (minced)
- **For Garnish:**
    - Sliced green onions
    - Sesame seeds (optional)

Instructions:

1. **Prepare the Pork:**
    - In a large bowl, mix flour, cornstarch, salt, and pepper. In a separate bowl, whisk the egg with cold water.
    - Dredge the pork cubes in the flour mixture, then dip into the egg mixture, and then dredge again in the flour mixture to coat thoroughly.
2. **Fry the Pork:**
    - Heat vegetable oil in a deep pan or fryer to 350°F (175°C). Fry the pork in batches until golden brown and crispy, about 4-5 minutes per batch. Remove with a slotted spoon and drain on paper towels.
3. **Prepare the Sauce:**

- In a medium saucepan, combine ketchup, rice vinegar, soy sauce, sugar, and pineapple juice. Bring to a simmer over medium heat.
- Stir in the cornstarch slurry and cook for 1-2 minutes, or until the sauce has thickened. Set aside.

4. **Stir-Fry Vegetables:**
    - In a large skillet or wok, heat 2 tablespoons vegetable oil over medium-high heat.
    - Add bell peppers and onion, and stir-fry for 2-3 minutes until they start to soften.
    - Add minced garlic and ginger, and stir-fry for another 1-2 minutes.
5. **Combine Pork and Sauce:**
    - Add the pineapple chunks and fried pork to the skillet with the vegetables.
    - Pour the prepared sauce over the pork and vegetables. Toss to coat everything evenly and heat through.
6. **Serve:**
    - Transfer the Sweet and Sour Pork to a serving dish. Garnish with sliced green onions and sesame seeds if desired.
    - Serve hot with steamed rice or noodles.

Enjoy your tangy, sweet, and savory Sweet and Sour Pork!

Mongolian Beef

Ingredients:

- **For the Beef:**
    - 1 lb (450g) flank steak (sliced thinly against the grain)
    - 1/4 cup cornstarch
    - 2 tablespoons vegetable oil (for frying)
- **For the Sauce:**
    - 1/2 cup soy sauce
    - 1/2 cup brown sugar
    - 1/4 cup water
    - 2 tablespoons hoisin sauce
    - 1 tablespoon rice vinegar
    - 1 tablespoon minced ginger
    - 3 cloves garlic (minced)
    - 1/4 teaspoon red pepper flakes (optional, for heat)
    - 1 tablespoon cornstarch mixed with 2 tablespoons water (cornstarch slurry)
- **For Stir-Frying:**
    - 2 tablespoons vegetable oil
    - 1 cup sliced green onions (both white and green parts)
    - 1/2 cup thinly sliced bell peppers (optional)
    - 1 tablespoon minced garlic
    - 1 tablespoon minced ginger

Instructions:

1. **Prepare the Beef:**
    - Toss the thinly sliced beef with cornstarch until evenly coated. Shake off excess cornstarch.
2. **Fry the Beef:**
    - Heat 2 tablespoons of vegetable oil in a large skillet or wok over medium-high heat.
    - Add the beef in batches (do not overcrowd) and stir-fry until browned and crispy, about 2-3 minutes per batch. Remove beef and set aside.
3. **Prepare the Sauce:**
    - In a bowl, mix soy sauce, brown sugar, water, hoisin sauce, rice vinegar, minced ginger, garlic, and red pepper flakes (if using). Set aside.
4. **Stir-Fry Vegetables:**
    - In the same skillet, add 2 tablespoons of vegetable oil. Add the sliced green onions, bell peppers (if using), minced garlic, and ginger. Stir-fry for 2-3 minutes until fragrant and slightly tender.
5. **Combine Beef and Sauce:**
    - Return the fried beef to the skillet. Pour the sauce over the beef and vegetables.

- Stir in the cornstarch slurry and cook for 1-2 minutes, or until the sauce thickens and coats the beef evenly.
6. **Serve:**
    - Transfer the Mongolian Beef to a serving dish. Garnish with extra green onions if desired.
    - Serve hot with steamed rice or noodles.

Enjoy your delicious and savory Mongolian Beef!

Lemon Chicken

Ingredients:

- **For the Chicken:**
    - 1 lb (450g) boneless, skinless chicken breasts or thighs (cut into bite-sized pieces)
    - 1/2 cup all-purpose flour
    - 1/2 cup cornstarch
    - 1/2 teaspoon baking powder
    - 1/2 teaspoon salt
    - 1/2 teaspoon ground black pepper
    - 1 egg
    - 1/2 cup cold water
    - Vegetable oil (for frying)
- **For the Lemon Sauce:**
    - 1/2 cup chicken broth
    - 1/4 cup lemon juice (freshly squeezed)
    - 1/4 cup sugar
    - 1 tablespoon soy sauce
    - 1 tablespoon cornstarch mixed with 2 tablespoons water (cornstarch slurry)
    - 1 tablespoon rice vinegar
    - 1 tablespoon lemon zest (optional, for extra lemon flavor)
- **For Stir-Frying:**
    - 2 tablespoons vegetable oil
    - 1/2 cup sliced bell peppers (red or green)
    - 1/2 cup sliced onions
    - 1 tablespoon minced garlic
    - 1 tablespoon minced ginger
- **For Garnish:**
    - Sliced green onions
    - Lemon wedges (optional)

Instructions:

1. **Prepare the Chicken:**
    - In a bowl, combine flour, cornstarch, baking powder, salt, and pepper. In a separate bowl, whisk the egg with cold water.
    - Coat the chicken pieces in the flour mixture, then dip into the egg mixture, and then dredge again in the flour mixture.
2. **Fry the Chicken:**
    - Heat vegetable oil in a deep pan or fryer to 350°F (175°C). Fry the chicken pieces in batches until golden brown and crispy, about 4-5 minutes per batch. Remove with a slotted spoon and drain on paper towels.

3. **Prepare the Lemon Sauce:**
     - In a medium saucepan, combine chicken broth, lemon juice, sugar, soy sauce, and rice vinegar. Bring to a simmer over medium heat.
     - Stir in the cornstarch slurry and cook for 1-2 minutes, or until the sauce has thickened. Add lemon zest if using.
4. **Stir-Fry Vegetables:**
     - In a large skillet or wok, heat 2 tablespoons vegetable oil over medium-high heat.
     - Add sliced bell peppers and onions, and stir-fry for 2-3 minutes until they start to soften.
     - Add minced garlic and ginger, and stir-fry for another 1-2 minutes.
5. **Combine Chicken and Sauce:**
     - Add the fried chicken pieces to the skillet with the vegetables.
     - Pour the lemon sauce over the chicken and vegetables. Toss to coat everything evenly and heat through.
6. **Serve:**
     - Transfer the Lemon Chicken to a serving dish. Garnish with sliced green onions and lemon wedges if desired.
     - Serve hot with steamed rice or noodles.

Enjoy your tangy and flavorful Lemon Chicken!

Beef and Broccoli

Ingredients:

- **For the Beef Marinade:**
    - 1 lb (450g) flank steak or sirloin (sliced thinly against the grain)
    - 1 tablespoon soy sauce
    - 1 tablespoon rice wine or dry sherry
    - 1 tablespoon cornstarch
    - 1 teaspoon vegetable oil
- **For the Stir-Fry:**
    - 2 tablespoons vegetable oil
    - 2 cups broccoli florets
    - 1/2 cup water (or chicken broth)
    - 1 tablespoon minced garlic
    - 1 tablespoon minced ginger
    - 1/4 cup sliced onions (optional)
    - 1/4 cup sliced carrots (optional)
- **For the Sauce:**
    - 1/4 cup soy sauce
    - 1/4 cup oyster sauce
    - 2 tablespoons hoisin sauce
    - 2 tablespoons brown sugar
    - 1/2 cup beef broth or water
    - 1 tablespoon cornstarch mixed with 2 tablespoons water (cornstarch slurry)
    - 1 teaspoon sesame oil
- **For Garnish:**
    - Sliced green onions
    - Sesame seeds (optional)

Instructions:

1. **Marinate the Beef:**
    - In a bowl, combine soy sauce, rice wine or sherry, cornstarch, and vegetable oil. Add the sliced beef and toss to coat. Let it marinate for at least 15 minutes.
2. **Prepare the Sauce:**
    - In a bowl, mix together soy sauce, oyster sauce, hoisin sauce, brown sugar, and beef broth or water. Stir in the cornstarch slurry and set aside.
3. **Blanch the Broccoli:**
    - In a large pot of boiling water, blanch the broccoli florets for 2-3 minutes until bright green and tender-crisp. Drain and set aside.
4. **Stir-Fry the Beef:**
    - Heat 2 tablespoons vegetable oil in a large skillet or wok over medium-high heat.

- Add the marinated beef in batches (do not overcrowd) and stir-fry until browned and cooked through, about 2-3 minutes per batch. Remove beef and set aside.
5. **Stir-Fry Vegetables:**
    - In the same skillet, add a bit more oil if needed. Add minced garlic, ginger, and optional onions and carrots. Stir-fry for 1-2 minutes until fragrant and slightly tender.
    - Add the blanched broccoli and stir to combine.
6. **Combine Beef and Sauce:**
    - Return the cooked beef to the skillet. Pour the prepared sauce over the beef and vegetables. Stir to coat everything evenly.
    - Cook for an additional 2-3 minutes, or until the sauce has thickened and everything is heated through.
7. **Serve:**
    - Transfer the Beef and Broccoli to a serving dish. Garnish with sliced green onions and sesame seeds if desired.
    - Serve hot with steamed rice.

Enjoy your savory and satisfying Beef and Broccoli!

Orange Chicken

Ingredients:

- **For the Chicken:**
    - 1 lb (450g) boneless, skinless chicken breasts or thighs (cut into bite-sized pieces)
    - 1/2 cup all-purpose flour
    - 1/2 cup cornstarch
    - 1/2 teaspoon baking powder
    - 1/2 teaspoon salt
    - 1/2 teaspoon ground black pepper
    - 1 egg
    - 1/2 cup cold water
    - Vegetable oil (for frying)
- **For the Orange Sauce:**
    - 1/2 cup fresh orange juice (about 2 oranges)
    - 1/4 cup soy sauce
    - 1/4 cup rice vinegar
    - 1/4 cup sugar
    - 1 tablespoon hoisin sauce
    - 1 tablespoon cornstarch mixed with 2 tablespoons water (cornstarch slurry)
    - 1 tablespoon minced ginger
    - 2 cloves garlic (minced)
    - 1 tablespoon orange zest (optional, for extra orange flavor)
    - 1/4 teaspoon crushed red pepper flakes (optional, for heat)
- **For Garnish:**
    - Sliced green onions
    - Sesame seeds (optional)
    - Orange slices (optional)

Instructions:

1. **Prepare the Chicken:**
    - In a bowl, combine flour, cornstarch, baking powder, salt, and pepper. In a separate bowl, whisk the egg with cold water.
    - Coat the chicken pieces in the flour mixture, then dip into the egg mixture, and then dredge again in the flour mixture.
2. **Fry the Chicken:**
    - Heat vegetable oil in a deep pan or fryer to 350°F (175°C). Fry the chicken pieces in batches until golden brown and crispy, about 4-5 minutes per batch. Remove with a slotted spoon and drain on paper towels.
3. **Prepare the Orange Sauce:**

- In a medium saucepan, combine orange juice, soy sauce, rice vinegar, sugar, hoisin sauce, minced ginger, garlic, and orange zest (if using). Bring to a simmer over medium heat.
- Stir in the cornstarch slurry and cook for 1-2 minutes, or until the sauce has thickened. Add red pepper flakes if using.

4. **Combine Chicken and Sauce:**
   - In a large skillet or wok, heat a small amount of oil if needed. Add the fried chicken pieces.
   - Pour the orange sauce over the chicken and toss to coat evenly. Cook for an additional 1-2 minutes to ensure the chicken is well coated and heated through.

5. **Serve:**
   - Transfer the Orange Chicken to a serving dish. Garnish with sliced green onions, sesame seeds, and orange slices if desired.
   - Serve hot with steamed rice or noodles.

Enjoy your tangy, sweet, and crispy Orange Chicken!

Szechuan Shrimp
Ingredients:

For the Shrimp:

1 lb (450g) large shrimp (peeled and deveined)
1 tablespoon soy sauce
1 tablespoon rice wine or dry sherry
1 tablespoon cornstarch
For the Sauce:

1/4 cup soy sauce
2 tablespoons rice vinegar
2 tablespoons hoisin sauce
2 tablespoons sugar
1 tablespoon chili paste or Szechuan peppercorn paste (adjust to taste)
1/2 cup chicken broth or water
1 tablespoon cornstarch mixed with 2 tablespoons water (cornstarch slurry)
1 tablespoon sesame oil
For Stir-Frying:

2 tablespoons vegetable oil
1 bell pepper (red or green, sliced)
1 onion (sliced)
3 cloves garlic (minced)
1 tablespoon fresh ginger (minced)
2-3 dried red chilies (optional, for extra heat)
1/4 cup sliced green onions (for garnish)
1 tablespoon sesame seeds (optional, for garnish)
Instructions:

Marinate the Shrimp:

In a bowl, combine shrimp with soy sauce, rice wine, and cornstarch. Mix well and let it marinate for about 15 minutes.
Prepare the Sauce:

In a bowl, mix together soy sauce, rice vinegar, hoisin sauce, sugar, chili paste or Szechuan peppercorn paste, and chicken broth or water. Stir in the cornstarch slurry and set aside.
Stir-Fry the Shrimp:

Heat 2 tablespoons vegetable oil in a large skillet or wok over medium-high heat.

Add the marinated shrimp and stir-fry for 2-3 minutes until they turn pink and are cooked through. Remove shrimp from the skillet and set aside.
Stir-Fry Vegetables:

In the same skillet, add a bit more oil if needed. Add sliced bell pepper, onion, dried red chilies (if using), minced garlic, and ginger. Stir-fry for 2-3 minutes until vegetables are tender-crisp.
Combine Shrimp and Sauce:

Return the cooked shrimp to the skillet. Pour the prepared sauce over the shrimp and vegetables.
Toss to coat everything evenly and cook for 1-2 minutes until the sauce has thickened and everything is heated through.
Serve:

Transfer the Szechuan Shrimp to a serving dish. Garnish with sliced green onions and sesame seeds if desired.
Serve hot with steamed rice or noodles.
Enjoy your spicy and aromatic Szechuan Shrimp!

Mapo Tofu

Ingredients:

- **For the Sauce:**
    - 1/4 cup doubanjiang (Sichuan broad bean paste)
    - 1 tablespoon douchi (fermented black beans, optional, finely chopped)
    - 2 tablespoons soy sauce
    - 1 tablespoon rice wine or dry sherry
    - 1 tablespoon hoisin sauce
    - 1 cup chicken broth or water
    - 1 tablespoon cornstarch mixed with 2 tablespoons water (cornstarch slurry)
    - 1 teaspoon sugar
- **For the Stir-Fry:**
    - 2 tablespoons vegetable oil
    - 1/2 lb (225g) ground pork (or beef, optional)
    - 3 cloves garlic (minced)
    - 1 tablespoon fresh ginger (minced)
    - 1 tablespoon Sichuan peppercorns (optional, for a numbing heat)
    - 1 cup water or chicken broth (for blanching tofu)
    - 1/2 cup scallions (chopped, for garnish)
    - 1 tablespoon sesame oil
- **For the Tofu:**
    - 1 block (14 oz) firm tofu (cubed)
    - Salt (to taste)

Instructions:

1. **Prepare the Tofu:**
    - Blanch the cubed tofu: In a pot, bring 1 cup of water or chicken broth to a boil. Add a pinch of salt and the cubed tofu. Cook for about 1-2 minutes, then drain and set aside.
2. **Prepare the Sauce:**
    - In a bowl, combine doubanjiang, douchi (if using), soy sauce, rice wine, hoisin sauce, and chicken broth or water. Stir in the cornstarch slurry and set aside.
3. **Stir-Fry:**
    - Heat vegetable oil in a large skillet or wok over medium-high heat.
    - Add ground pork (if using) and cook until browned and crispy, breaking it apart as it cooks. Remove excess fat if necessary.
    - Add minced garlic, ginger, and Sichuan peppercorns (if using) to the skillet. Stir-fry for 1-2 minutes until fragrant.
4. **Combine Tofu and Sauce:**
    - Add the prepared sauce to the skillet and bring to a simmer.

- Gently add the blanched tofu cubes to the skillet. Stir gently to coat the tofu with the sauce without breaking the cubes.
- Simmer for 3-5 minutes, allowing the tofu to absorb the flavors and the sauce to thicken.

5. **Finish and Serve:**
    - Stir in sesame oil and adjust seasoning with salt if needed.
    - Garnish with chopped scallions.
    - Serve hot with steamed rice.

Enjoy your spicy and savory Mapo Tofu!

Hot and Sour Soup

Ingredients:

- **For the Soup:**
    - 4 cups chicken broth or vegetable broth
    - 1/2 cup sliced shiitake mushrooms (or other mushrooms)
    - 1/2 cup sliced bamboo shoots (canned or fresh)
    - 1/2 cup sliced wood ear mushrooms (optional, soaked if dried)
    - 1/2 cup tofu (cubed, firm or extra-firm)
    - 1/2 cup sliced pork (optional, thinly sliced)
    - 2 tablespoons soy sauce
    - 2 tablespoons rice vinegar
    - 1 tablespoon white vinegar (for extra tang)
    - 1 tablespoon hoisin sauce (optional, for added depth)
    - 1 tablespoon cornstarch mixed with 2 tablespoons water (cornstarch slurry)
    - 2 teaspoons sesame oil
    - 2 large eggs (beaten)
    - 1/4 teaspoon white pepper (adjust to taste)
    - 1/4 teaspoon ground black pepper
    - 1/2 teaspoon sugar (optional, to balance the flavors)
- **For Garnish:**
    - Sliced green onions
    - Fresh cilantro (optional)
    - Extra white pepper (to taste)
    - Additional vinegar (optional, for extra tang)

Instructions:

1. **Prepare the Ingredients:**
    - Slice the mushrooms, bamboo shoots, and tofu. Thinly slice the pork if using.
2. **Start the Soup:**
    - In a large pot, bring the chicken or vegetable broth to a boil over medium-high heat.
3. **Add the Ingredients:**
    - Add the mushrooms, bamboo shoots, wood ear mushrooms (if using), tofu, and sliced pork (if using) to the pot.
    - Stir in soy sauce, rice vinegar, white vinegar, and hoisin sauce (if using). Let it simmer for 3-5 minutes.
4. **Thicken the Soup:**
    - Stir in the cornstarch slurry and continue to simmer until the soup slightly thickens, about 1-2 minutes.
5. **Add Eggs:**

    - Slowly drizzle the beaten eggs into the simmering soup while stirring gently to create egg ribbons.
6. **Season:**
    - Stir in sesame oil, white pepper, black pepper, and sugar (if using). Adjust seasoning with additional vinegar or pepper to taste.
7. **Serve:**
    - Ladle the soup into bowls. Garnish with sliced green onions and fresh cilantro if desired.

Enjoy your hot and tangy Hot and Sour Soup!

Wonton Soup

Ingredients:

- **For the Wontons:**
    - 1/2 lb (225g) ground pork (or a mix of pork and shrimp)
    - 1/2 cup finely chopped shrimp (optional, for added flavor)
    - 1/4 cup finely chopped water chestnuts or bamboo shoots (optional, for crunch)
    - 2 tablespoons soy sauce
    - 1 tablespoon oyster sauce
    - 1 tablespoon rice wine or dry sherry
    - 1 teaspoon sesame oil
    - 1 teaspoon grated ginger
    - 1 garlic clove (minced)
    - 1/4 cup chopped green onions
    - 1 package wonton wrappers (about 30-40 wrappers)
    - 1 egg (beaten, for sealing the wrappers)
- **For the Soup:**
    - 6 cups chicken broth or vegetable broth
    - 2 cups water
    - 2 tablespoons soy sauce
    - 1 tablespoon rice wine or dry sherry
    - 1 teaspoon sesame oil
    - 1 cup baby bok choy or spinach (chopped, optional)
    - 1/4 cup sliced mushrooms (shiitake or button, optional)
    - 2 garlic cloves (minced)
    - 1 tablespoon fresh ginger (sliced thinly)
    - Salt and pepper to taste
- **For Garnish:**
    - Sliced green onions
    - Fresh cilantro (optional)
    - Chili oil or soy sauce (optional, for extra flavor)

Instructions:

1. **Prepare the Wonton Filling:**
    - In a bowl, combine ground pork, chopped shrimp (if using), chopped water chestnuts or bamboo shoots (if using), soy sauce, oyster sauce, rice wine, sesame oil, grated ginger, minced garlic, and chopped green onions. Mix well.
2. **Assemble the Wontons:**
    - Place a small teaspoon of filling in the center of each wonton wrapper.
    - Brush the edges of the wrapper with beaten egg.

- Fold the wrapper over the filling to form a triangle or rectangle and press the edges to seal. You can also bring the corners of the wrapper together to form a pouch, if desired.
3. **Cook the Wontons:**
    - Bring a large pot of water to a boil. Add the wontons in batches, cooking for about 3-4 minutes or until they float to the top and are cooked through. Remove with a slotted spoon and set aside.
4. **Prepare the Soup Base:**
    - In a large pot, combine chicken or vegetable broth, water, soy sauce, rice wine, and sesame oil. Add the garlic, sliced ginger, and optional mushrooms.
    - Bring to a boil and then simmer for 5-10 minutes to develop the flavors. Add chopped baby bok choy or spinach if using and cook for an additional 1-2 minutes.
5. **Combine Wontons and Soup:**
    - Gently add the cooked wontons to the soup. Simmer for a few minutes until everything is heated through.
6. **Serve:**
    - Ladle the soup and wontons into bowls. Garnish with sliced green onions and fresh cilantro if desired. Drizzle with chili oil or soy sauce for extra flavor if you like.

Enjoy your comforting and delicious Wonton Soup!

Egg Drop Soup

Ingredients:

- **For the Soup:**
    - 4 cups chicken broth or vegetable broth
    - 1 cup water
    - 1 tablespoon soy sauce
    - 1 teaspoon sesame oil
    - 1 tablespoon cornstarch mixed with 2 tablespoons water (cornstarch slurry)
    - 2 large eggs (beaten)
    - 1/4 cup sliced mushrooms (shiitake, button, or your choice, optional)
    - 1/2 cup frozen or fresh peas (optional)
    - 1/4 cup sliced green onions
    - 1/2 teaspoon white pepper (adjust to taste)
    - 1/4 teaspoon salt (or to taste)
- **For Garnish:**
    - Sliced green onions
    - Fresh cilantro (optional)
    - A drizzle of sesame oil (optional)

Instructions:

1. **Prepare the Soup Base:**
    - In a large pot, combine chicken or vegetable broth and water. Bring to a boil over medium-high heat.
2. **Thicken the Broth:**
    - Stir in the cornstarch slurry (cornstarch mixed with water) to the boiling broth. This will help to slightly thicken the soup. Let it simmer for a few minutes until the broth starts to thicken.
3. **Add Flavorings:**
    - Add soy sauce, sesame oil, white pepper, and salt to the broth. Adjust seasoning to taste.
4. **Add Optional Ingredients:**
    - If using mushrooms or peas, add them to the pot and let them cook for a few minutes until tender.
5. **Create the Egg Ribbons:**
    - Reduce the heat to low. Gently stir the soup in a circular motion to create a whirlpool effect. Slowly pour the beaten eggs into the swirling broth in a thin stream, stirring gently as you pour. This will create delicate egg ribbons in the soup.
6. **Finish and Serve:**
    - Once the eggs are cooked and have formed ribbons, remove the pot from the heat.

- Ladle the soup into bowls and garnish with sliced green onions and fresh cilantro if desired.
- Drizzle a little sesame oil on top for extra flavor if you like.

Enjoy your warm and comforting Egg Drop Soup!

Fried Rice

Ingredients:

- **For the Fried Rice:**
    - 2 cups cooked rice (preferably cold and day-old; jasmine or long-grain rice works best)
    - 2 tablespoons vegetable oil
    - 1/2 cup diced onion
    - 2 cloves garlic (minced)
    - 1/2 cup diced carrots
    - 1/2 cup frozen peas
    - 1/2 cup diced bell pepper (any color)
    - 2 large eggs (beaten)
    - 1 cup cooked chicken, shrimp, or pork (optional, diced)
    - 2-3 green onions (sliced)
    - 3 tablespoons soy sauce (adjust to taste)
    - 1 tablespoon oyster sauce (optional, for extra depth)
    - 1 teaspoon sesame oil
    - Salt and pepper to taste
- **For Garnish (optional):**
    - Extra sliced green onions
    - Sesame seeds

Instructions:

1. **Prepare Ingredients:**
    - Ensure the rice is cold and separated. Chop all vegetables and proteins as needed.
2. **Cook the Vegetables:**
    - Heat vegetable oil in a large skillet or wok over medium-high heat.
    - Add diced onion and cook until translucent, about 2-3 minutes.
    - Add minced garlic and cook for another 30 seconds until fragrant.
    - Add diced carrots and bell pepper. Stir-fry for 3-4 minutes until vegetables are tender-crisp.
    - Stir in the frozen peas and cook for an additional 1-2 minutes.
3. **Cook the Eggs:**
    - Push the vegetables to one side of the skillet or wok. Add a little more oil if needed.
    - Pour the beaten eggs into the empty side of the skillet. Scramble and cook until just set, then mix with the vegetables.
4. **Add Protein (if using):**
    - Add the cooked chicken, shrimp, or pork (if using) to the skillet. Stir to combine and heat through.

5. **Add Rice and Seasonings:**
    - Add the cold rice to the skillet. Break up any clumps and mix well with the vegetables and eggs.
    - Stir in soy sauce, oyster sauce (if using), and sesame oil. Mix thoroughly until the rice is evenly coated and heated through.
    - Season with salt and pepper to taste.
6. **Finish and Serve:**
    - Stir in sliced green onions.
    - Garnish with additional green onions and sesame seeds if desired.

Enjoy your homemade Fried Rice! It's a great dish to customize with your favorite ingredients and is perfect as a main or side dish.

Lo Mein

Ingredients:

- **For the Lo Mein:**
    - 8 oz (225g) fresh or dried lo mein noodles (or substitute with egg noodles or spaghetti)
    - 2 tablespoons vegetable oil
    - 1/2 cup sliced onion
    - 2 cloves garlic (minced)
    - 1 cup sliced bell peppers (any color)
    - 1 cup sliced mushrooms (shiitake or button)
    - 1 cup shredded carrots
    - 1/2 cup snow peas or snap peas
    - 1 cup cooked chicken, beef, shrimp, or tofu (diced, optional)
    - 2-3 green onions (sliced)
- **For the Sauce:**
    - 1/4 cup soy sauce
    - 2 tablespoons oyster sauce (optional, for added depth)
    - 1 tablespoon hoisin sauce
    - 1 tablespoon rice vinegar
    - 1 tablespoon sesame oil
    - 1 tablespoon brown sugar
    - 1 teaspoon cornstarch mixed with 1 tablespoon water (cornstarch slurry)
- **For Garnish (optional):**
    - Sesame seeds
    - Additional sliced green onions

Instructions:

1. **Prepare the Noodles:**
    - Cook the lo mein noodles according to the package instructions. Drain and set aside. If using dried noodles, be sure to rinse them under cold water to prevent sticking.
2. **Prepare the Sauce:**
    - In a small bowl, mix together soy sauce, oyster sauce (if using), hoisin sauce, rice vinegar, sesame oil, brown sugar, and cornstarch slurry. Set aside.
3. **Stir-Fry the Vegetables:**
    - Heat vegetable oil in a large skillet or wok over medium-high heat.
    - Add sliced onion and cook until translucent, about 2-3 minutes.
    - Add minced garlic and cook for another 30 seconds until fragrant.
    - Add sliced bell peppers, mushrooms, and shredded carrots. Stir-fry for 3-4 minutes until vegetables are tender-crisp.
    - Add snow peas or snap peas and cook for an additional 1-2 minutes.

4. **Add Protein (if using):**
    - Add the cooked chicken, beef, shrimp, or tofu to the skillet. Stir to combine and heat through.
5. **Combine Noodles and Sauce:**
    - Add the cooked noodles to the skillet. Pour the prepared sauce over the noodles and vegetables.
    - Toss everything together until the noodles are evenly coated with the sauce and heated through.
6. **Finish and Serve:**
    - Stir in sliced green onions.
    - Garnish with sesame seeds and additional green onions if desired.

Enjoy your delicious and customizable Lo Mein! It's perfect as a quick meal or side dish and can be tailored to your taste with different vegetables and proteins.

Chow Mein

Ingredients:

- **For the Chow Mein:**
  - 8 oz (225g) fresh or dried chow mein noodles (or substitute with egg noodles or spaghetti)
  - 2 tablespoons vegetable oil
  - 1/2 cup sliced onion
  - 2 cloves garlic (minced)
  - 1 cup sliced bell peppers (any color)
  - 1 cup sliced mushrooms (shiitake, button, or your choice)
  - 1 cup shredded carrots
  - 1/2 cup snap peas or snow peas
  - 1 cup cooked chicken, beef, shrimp, or tofu (diced, optional)
  - 2-3 green onions (sliced)
- **For the Sauce:**
  - 1/4 cup soy sauce
  - 2 tablespoons oyster sauce (optional, for added depth)
  - 1 tablespoon hoisin sauce
  - 1 tablespoon rice vinegar
  - 1 tablespoon sesame oil
  - 1 tablespoon brown sugar
  - 1 teaspoon cornstarch mixed with 1 tablespoon water (cornstarch slurry)
- **For Garnish (optional):**
  - Sesame seeds
  - Additional sliced green onions

Instructions:

1. **Prepare the Noodles:**
   - Cook the chow mein noodles according to the package instructions. Drain and set aside. If using dried noodles, rinse under cold water to prevent sticking.
2. **Prepare the Sauce:**
   - In a small bowl, mix together soy sauce, oyster sauce (if using), hoisin sauce, rice vinegar, sesame oil, brown sugar, and cornstarch slurry. Set aside.
3. **Stir-Fry the Vegetables:**
   - Heat vegetable oil in a large skillet or wok over medium-high heat.
   - Add sliced onion and cook until translucent, about 2-3 minutes.
   - Add minced garlic and cook for another 30 seconds until fragrant.
   - Add sliced bell peppers, mushrooms, and shredded carrots. Stir-fry for 3-4 minutes until vegetables are tender-crisp.
   - Add snap peas or snow peas and cook for an additional 1-2 minutes.
4. **Add Protein (if using):**

- Add the cooked chicken, beef, shrimp, or tofu to the skillet. Stir to combine and heat through.

5. **Combine Noodles and Sauce:**
   - Add the cooked noodles to the skillet. Pour the prepared sauce over the noodles and vegetables.
   - Toss everything together until the noodles are evenly coated with the sauce and heated through.

6. **Finish and Serve:**
   - Stir in sliced green onions.
   - Garnish with sesame seeds and additional green onions if desired.

Enjoy your flavorful and crispy Chow Mein! It's a great dish for a quick weeknight dinner and can be customized with your favorite vegetables and proteins.

Dumplings

Ingredients:

- **For the Dumpling Dough:**
    - 2 cups all-purpose flour
    - 1 cup boiling water
    - 1/4 teaspoon salt
- **For the Filling:**
    - 1/2 lb (225g) ground pork (or chicken, beef, or tofu)
    - 1 cup finely chopped cabbage
    - 1/2 cup finely chopped mushrooms (shiitake or button)
    - 2 green onions (chopped)
    - 2 cloves garlic (minced)
    - 1 tablespoon ginger (minced)
    - 2 tablespoons soy sauce
    - 1 tablespoon oyster sauce (optional)
    - 1 tablespoon sesame oil
    - 1 teaspoon sugar
    - 1/2 teaspoon white pepper (adjust to taste)
    - 1 egg (optional, for binding the filling)
- **For Cooking:**
    - Vegetable oil (for pan-frying)
    - Water (for steaming or boiling)
- **For Dipping Sauce (optional):**
    - 2 tablespoons soy sauce
    - 1 tablespoon rice vinegar
    - 1 teaspoon sesame oil
    - 1/2 teaspoon sugar
    - 1 clove garlic (minced, optional)
    - 1 teaspoon chili oil or hot sauce (optional, for heat)

Instructions:

1. **Prepare the Dumpling Dough:**
    - In a large bowl, combine flour and salt.
    - Gradually add boiling water to the flour while stirring with a fork or chopsticks until the mixture starts to come together.
    - When the dough is cool enough to handle, knead it on a floured surface until smooth, about 5-7 minutes.
    - Cover the dough with a damp cloth or plastic wrap and let it rest for at least 30 minutes.
2. **Prepare the Filling:**

- In a large bowl, combine ground pork, chopped cabbage, mushrooms, green onions, garlic, ginger, soy sauce, oyster sauce (if using), sesame oil, sugar, and white pepper. Mix well.
- If using, mix in the egg to help bind the filling.

3. **Assemble the Dumplings:**
   - Roll out the rested dough on a floured surface into a thin sheet. Use a round cutter (about 3-4 inches in diameter) or a glass to cut out circles.
   - Place a small spoonful of filling in the center of each dough circle.
   - Moisten the edges of the dough with water. Fold the dough over the filling to create a half-moon shape. Pinch the edges to seal, pleating the edges if desired.

4. **Cook the Dumplings:**

   Steamed:
   - Place dumplings on a parchment-lined steaming rack, making sure they are not touching.
   - Steam over boiling water for about 10-12 minutes, or until the dough is translucent and the filling is cooked through.

5. **Boiled:**
   - Bring a large pot of water to a boil.
   - Add dumplings in batches, stirring gently to prevent sticking.
   - Boil for about 5-7 minutes, or until they float to the surface and are cooked through. Remove with a slotted spoon.

6. **Pan-Fried (Potstickers):**
   - Heat a little vegetable oil in a skillet over medium-high heat.
   - Add dumplings and cook until the bottoms are golden brown, about 2-3 minutes.
   - Carefully add 1/4 cup of water to the skillet, cover immediately, and steam for about 5-7 minutes, or until the water has evaporated and the dumplings are cooked through.

7. **Prepare the Dipping Sauce (optional):**
   - In a small bowl, mix soy sauce, rice vinegar, sesame oil, sugar, garlic (if using), and chili oil or hot sauce (if using).

8. **Serve:**
   - Serve dumplings hot with the dipping sauce on the side.

Enjoy your homemade dumplings, whether you like them steamed, boiled, or pan-fried!

Spring Rolls

Ingredients:

- **For the Filling:**
    - 1/2 lb (225g) ground pork (or chicken, shrimp, or tofu)
    - 1 cup shredded cabbage
    - 1/2 cup shredded carrots
    - 1/2 cup sliced mushrooms (shiitake or button)
    - 1/4 cup bean sprouts
    - 2 cloves garlic (minced)
    - 1 tablespoon ginger (minced)
    - 2 tablespoons soy sauce
    - 1 tablespoon oyster sauce (optional)
    - 1 tablespoon hoisin sauce (optional)
    - 1 teaspoon sesame oil
    - 1/2 teaspoon white pepper
    - 1/4 teaspoon salt
- **For Rolling:**
    - Spring roll wrappers (available in the frozen section of Asian grocery stores, usually 8-10 inches in diameter)
    - 1 egg (beaten, for sealing)
    - Vegetable oil (for frying, if desired)
- **For Dipping Sauce (optional):**
    - 1/4 cup soy sauce
    - 2 tablespoons rice vinegar
    - 1 tablespoon honey or sugar
    - 1 teaspoon sesame oil
    - 1 clove garlic (minced, optional)
    - 1 teaspoon chili oil or hot sauce (optional, for heat)

Instructions:

1. **Prepare the Filling:**
    - Heat a large skillet or wok over medium-high heat. Add a small amount of oil.
    - Add the ground pork (or your choice of protein) and cook until browned, breaking it up with a spoon as it cooks.
    - Add garlic and ginger. Cook for another minute until fragrant.
    - Add shredded cabbage, carrots, mushrooms, and bean sprouts. Stir-fry for 3-4 minutes until vegetables are tender.
    - Stir in soy sauce, oyster sauce, hoisin sauce (if using), sesame oil, white pepper, and salt. Cook for an additional 2-3 minutes, then remove from heat and let the filling cool.
2. **Prepare the Spring Rolls:**

- Place a spring roll wrapper on a clean surface with one corner pointing towards you (like a diamond shape).
- Spoon a small amount of filling (about 2 tablespoons) onto the bottom third of the wrapper.
- Fold the bottom corner over the filling, then fold in the sides, and roll up tightly to seal. Brush the top edge of the wrapper with a little beaten egg to seal the roll.
- Repeat with the remaining wrappers and filling.

3. **Fry the Spring Rolls (optional):**
   - Heat vegetable oil in a large skillet or wok over medium-high heat. The oil should be about 350°F (175°C).
   - Fry the spring rolls in batches, turning occasionally, until they are golden brown and crispy, about 3-4 minutes per batch.
   - Remove from oil and drain on paper towels.
4. **Serve Fresh or Fried:**
   - Fresh spring rolls can be served immediately with dipping sauce.
   - Fried spring rolls should be drained on paper towels and served hot.
5. **Prepare the Dipping Sauce (optional):**
   - In a small bowl, mix soy sauce, rice vinegar, honey or sugar, sesame oil, garlic (if using), and chili oil or hot sauce (if using).

Enjoy your delicious homemade Spring Rolls, whether you prefer them fresh and crisp or fried and golden!

Crab Rangoon

Ingredients:

- **For the Filling:**
    - 8 oz (225g) cream cheese (softened)
    - 1/2 cup cooked crab meat (imitation crab or real crab)
    - 1/4 cup finely chopped green onions
    - 1/4 cup finely chopped water chestnuts (optional, for crunch)
    - 1 clove garlic (minced)
    - 1 teaspoon soy sauce
    - 1 teaspoon Worcestershire sauce
    - 1/2 teaspoon sesame oil
    - 1/4 teaspoon salt
    - 1/4 teaspoon white pepper
- **For the Wrappers:**
    - 1 package wonton wrappers (about 30-40 wrappers)
    - Vegetable oil (for frying)
- **For Dipping Sauce (optional):**
    - 1/4 cup sweet and sour sauce
    - 1 tablespoon soy sauce
    - 1 tablespoon rice vinegar
    - 1 teaspoon honey or sugar

Instructions:

1. **Prepare the Filling:**
    - In a medium bowl, combine softened cream cheese, crab meat, green onions, water chestnuts (if using), minced garlic, soy sauce, Worcestershire sauce, sesame oil, salt, and white pepper.
    - Mix well until all ingredients are thoroughly combined.
2. **Assemble the Crab Rangoon:**
    - Place a small spoonful of the crab mixture in the center of each wonton wrapper.
    - Moisten the edges of the wrapper with a little water using your finger or a brush.
    - Fold the wrapper over the filling to form a triangle, pressing the edges to seal. You can also fold the edges into a small pouch or create a purse-like shape if you prefer.
    - Ensure that the edges are well-sealed to prevent the filling from leaking during frying.
3. **Fry the Crab Rangoon:**
    - Heat vegetable oil in a deep skillet or wok over medium-high heat to 350°F (175°C).
    - Fry the Crab Rangoon in batches, being careful not to overcrowd the pan. Fry until they are golden brown and crispy, about 2-3 minutes per batch.

- Remove with a slotted spoon and drain on paper towels.
4. **Prepare the Dipping Sauce (optional):**
    - In a small bowl, mix together sweet and sour sauce, soy sauce, rice vinegar, and honey or sugar.
5. **Serve:**
    - Serve the Crab Rangoon hot with the dipping sauce on the side.

Enjoy your homemade Crab Rangoon, perfect as an appetizer or snack!

Char Siu (BBQ Pork)

Ingredients:

- **For the Marinade:**
    - 1/2 cup hoisin sauce
    - 1/4 cup soy sauce
    - 1/4 cup honey
    - 2 tablespoons Chinese rice wine or dry sherry
    - 2 tablespoons sugar
    - 1 tablespoon dark soy sauce (for color)
    - 1 tablespoon five-spice powder
    - 1 tablespoon minced garlic
    - 1 tablespoon minced ginger
    - 1 teaspoon red food coloring (optional, for traditional color)
- **For the Pork:**
    - 1.5 lbs (680g) pork shoulder or pork loin, trimmed and cut into long strips
- **For Basting:**
    - 2 tablespoons honey mixed with 1 tablespoon water (for glazing)
    - 1 tablespoon soy sauce (for glazing)

Instructions:

1. **Prepare the Marinade:**
    - In a bowl, mix together hoisin sauce, soy sauce, honey, rice wine or dry sherry, sugar, dark soy sauce, five-spice powder, minced garlic, minced ginger, and red food coloring (if using).
    - Stir until the sugar is dissolved and the marinade is well combined.
2. **Marinate the Pork:**
    - Place the pork strips in a resealable plastic bag or a shallow dish.
    - Pour the marinade over the pork, ensuring that all pieces are well-coated.
    - Seal the bag or cover the dish and refrigerate for at least 4 hours, preferably overnight, to allow the flavors to penetrate the meat.
3. **Preheat the Oven:**
    - Preheat your oven to 375°F (190°C). Line a baking sheet with aluminum foil and place a rack on top of it.
4. **Roast the Pork:**
    - Remove the pork from the marinade and place the strips on the rack, allowing any excess marinade to drip off.
    - Roast in the preheated oven for about 25-30 minutes.
    - Baste the pork with the honey-water mixture and soy sauce every 10 minutes for a glossy finish and to keep it moist.
5. **Finish Roasting:**

- After 25-30 minutes, flip the pork strips and roast for an additional 15-20 minutes, or until the pork is cooked through and has a caramelized, slightly charred exterior.
6. **Rest and Slice:**
    - Remove the pork from the oven and let it rest for a few minutes before slicing.
    - Slice the Char Siu into thin strips or bite-sized pieces.
7. **Serve:**
    - Serve the Char Siu with steamed rice, noodles, or in a bao bun. It can also be added to stir-fries or used as a flavorful topping for various dishes.

Enjoy your homemade Char Siu, which brings the taste of classic Chinese BBQ right to your kitchen!

Ma Po Tofu

Ingredients:

- **For the Dish:**
    - 14 oz (400g) firm tofu (cut into 1-inch cubes)
    - 1/2 lb (225g) ground pork (or ground beef)
    - 2 tablespoons vegetable oil
    - 1/2 cup diced onion
    - 3 cloves garlic (minced)
    - 1 tablespoon ginger (minced)
    - 2 tablespoons doubanjiang (Sichuan chili bean paste)
    - 1 tablespoon fermented black beans (douchi, optional, rinsed and mashed)
    - 1 cup chicken or vegetable broth
    - 1 tablespoon soy sauce
    - 1 tablespoon rice wine or dry sherry
    - 1 teaspoon sugar
    - 1 tablespoon cornstarch mixed with 2 tablespoons water (cornstarch slurry)
    - 2 tablespoons sesame oil
    - 2 green onions (sliced, for garnish)
    - 1 teaspoon Sichuan peppercorns (optional, toasted and ground)
    - Cooked rice (for serving)

Instructions:

1. **Prepare the Tofu:**
    - Cut the tofu into 1-inch cubes. To remove excess moisture and make it more resilient, you can lightly pan-fry the tofu cubes in a non-stick skillet with a little oil over medium heat until golden brown on all sides. This step is optional but recommended for added texture.
2. **Cook the Pork:**
    - Heat vegetable oil in a large skillet or wok over medium-high heat.
    - Add diced onion and cook until translucent, about 2-3 minutes.
    - Add minced garlic and ginger, cooking for another 30 seconds until fragrant.
    - Add ground pork to the skillet. Cook until browned and cooked through, breaking it up with a spoon as it cooks.
3. **Add the Flavorings:**
    - Stir in doubanjiang (Sichuan chili bean paste) and fermented black beans (if using). Cook for 1-2 minutes, allowing the flavors to meld.
    - Add chicken or vegetable broth, soy sauce, rice wine or dry sherry, and sugar. Stir to combine and bring to a simmer.
4. **Add the Tofu:**
    - Gently add the tofu cubes to the skillet. Stir carefully to avoid breaking up the tofu.

- Simmer for about 5-7 minutes, allowing the tofu to absorb the flavors of the sauce.
5. **Thicken the Sauce:**
    - Stir in the cornstarch slurry and cook for an additional 1-2 minutes until the sauce thickens to your desired consistency.
6. **Finish the Dish:**
    - Stir in sesame oil and ground Sichuan peppercorns (if using) for added flavor.
    - Garnish with sliced green onions.
7. **Serve:**
    - Serve the Ma Po Tofu hot over steamed rice.

Enjoy your homemade Ma Po Tofu with its rich, spicy, and aromatic flavors that are characteristic of Sichuan cuisine!

Mongolian Beef

Ingredients:

- **For the Beef:**
    - 1 lb (450g) flank steak or sirloin, thinly sliced against the grain
    - 1/4 cup cornstarch
    - 2 tablespoons vegetable oil (for frying)
- **For the Sauce:**
    - 1/4 cup soy sauce
    - 1/4 cup hoisin sauce
    - 2 tablespoons oyster sauce
    - 2 tablespoons brown sugar
    - 1 tablespoon rice vinegar
    - 1 teaspoon sesame oil
    - 1/2 cup water
    - 1 tablespoon cornstarch mixed with 1 tablespoon water (cornstarch slurry)
- **For Stir-Frying:**
    - 2 tablespoons vegetable oil
    - 4 cloves garlic (minced)
    - 1 tablespoon ginger (minced)
    - 1-2 red or green chilies, sliced (optional, for heat)
    - 1 cup sliced green onions (white and green parts)

Instructions:

1. **Prepare the Beef:**
    - Place the thinly sliced beef in a bowl and toss with 1/4 cup cornstarch until the beef is evenly coated. This will help to crisp up the beef and thicken the sauce.
2. **Prepare the Sauce:**
    - In a bowl, whisk together soy sauce, hoisin sauce, oyster sauce, brown sugar, rice vinegar, sesame oil, and water.
    - Stir in the cornstarch slurry to thicken the sauce. Set aside.
3. **Cook the Beef:**
    - Heat 2 tablespoons vegetable oil in a large skillet or wok over medium-high heat.
    - Add the coated beef in batches, being careful not to overcrowd the pan. Cook until the beef is browned and crispy, about 2-3 minutes per side. Remove beef from the skillet and set aside.
4. **Stir-Fry the Aromatics:**
    - In the same skillet, add 2 tablespoons vegetable oil. Heat over medium heat.
    - Add minced garlic, ginger, and sliced chilies (if using). Stir-fry for about 30 seconds until fragrant.
5. **Combine Beef and Sauce:**
    - Return the cooked beef to the skillet with the aromatics.

- Pour the prepared sauce over the beef. Stir well to coat the beef in the sauce.
- Cook for another 2-3 minutes, allowing the sauce to thicken and coat the beef evenly.
6. **Add Green Onions:**
    - Stir in the sliced green onions and cook for an additional 1-2 minutes.
7. **Serve:**
    - Serve Mongolian Beef hot over steamed rice or noodles.

Enjoy your homemade Mongolian Beef, a dish that combines rich, savory flavors with a touch of sweetness for a satisfying meal!

Sichuan Spicy Noodles

Ingredients:

- **For the Noodles:**
    - 8 oz (225g) dried noodles (such as egg noodles or wheat noodles)
- **For the Sauce:**
    - 2 tablespoons Sichuan chili bean paste (doubanjiang)
    - 2 tablespoons soy sauce
    - 1 tablespoon rice vinegar
    - 1 tablespoon hoisin sauce
    - 1 tablespoon sesame paste or tahini
    - 1 tablespoon sugar
    - 2 tablespoons water
    - 1 teaspoon sesame oil
- **For the Toppings:**
    - 1/2 lb (225g) ground pork
    - 2 tablespoons vegetable oil
    - 2 cloves garlic (minced)
    - 1 tablespoon ginger (minced)
    - 1/4 cup chopped green onions (white and green parts)
    - 2 tablespoons Sichuan peppercorns (toasted and ground)
    - 1/4 cup roasted peanuts or sesame seeds (optional, for garnish)
    - 1/4 cup chopped cilantro (optional, for garnish)
- **For Serving:**
    - Additional chopped green onions
    - Additional chopped cilantro

Instructions:

1. **Cook the Noodles:**
    - Cook the dried noodles according to the package instructions. Drain and rinse under cold water to stop the cooking process. Set aside.
2. **Prepare the Sauce:**
    - In a bowl, combine Sichuan chili bean paste, soy sauce, rice vinegar, hoisin sauce, sesame paste or tahini, sugar, water, and sesame oil. Mix well until smooth and set aside.
3. **Cook the Pork:**
    - Heat vegetable oil in a large skillet or wok over medium-high heat.
    - Add ground pork and cook until browned and cooked through, breaking it up with a spoon as it cooks.
    - Add minced garlic and ginger to the skillet. Cook for an additional minute until fragrant.

- Stir in chopped green onions and ground Sichuan peppercorns. Cook for another 1-2 minutes.
4. **Combine Noodles and Sauce:**
    - Add the cooked noodles to the skillet with the pork mixture. Pour the prepared sauce over the noodles.
    - Toss everything together to ensure the noodles are well-coated with the sauce and heated through.
5. **Serve:**
    - Divide the noodles among serving bowls.
    - Garnish with roasted peanuts or sesame seeds and chopped cilantro, if desired.
    - Top with additional chopped green onions and cilantro for extra flavor.
6. **Optional:**
    - Adjust the level of spiciness by adding more Sichuan chili bean paste or chili oil if you prefer extra heat.

Enjoy your Sichuan Spicy Noodles, a dish that combines the vibrant flavors of Sichuan cuisine with the satisfying texture of noodles!

Beef with Black Bean Sauce

Ingredients:

- **For the Beef:**
    - 1 lb (450g) flank steak or sirloin, thinly sliced against the grain
    - 2 tablespoons cornstarch
    - 1 tablespoon soy sauce
- **For the Black Bean Sauce:**
    - 2 tablespoons fermented black beans (douchi), rinsed and mashed
    - 2 tablespoons oyster sauce
    - 1 tablespoon soy sauce
    - 1 tablespoon rice wine or dry sherry
    - 1 tablespoon hoisin sauce
    - 1 teaspoon sugar
    - 1/2 cup water or beef broth
- **For Stir-Frying:**
    - 2 tablespoons vegetable oil
    - 1 bell pepper, sliced
    - 1 onion, sliced
    - 2 cloves garlic, minced
    - 1 tablespoon ginger, minced
    - 1 cup snap peas or snow peas
    - 1 tablespoon cornstarch mixed with 2 tablespoons water (cornstarch slurry)
- **For Garnish (optional):**
    - Sliced green onions
    - Fresh cilantro

Instructions:

1. **Prepare the Beef:**
    - Toss the thinly sliced beef with cornstarch and soy sauce. Let it marinate for about 15 minutes. This helps tenderize the beef and gives it a nice coating for stir-frying.
2. **Prepare the Black Bean Sauce:**
    - In a bowl, mix together mashed fermented black beans, oyster sauce, soy sauce, rice wine or dry sherry, hoisin sauce, sugar, and water or beef broth. Stir well to combine. Set aside.
3. **Cook the Beef:**
    - Heat 2 tablespoons of vegetable oil in a large skillet or wok over medium-high heat.
    - Add the marinated beef and stir-fry until it's browned and just cooked through, about 2-3 minutes. Remove the beef from the skillet and set aside.
4. **Stir-Fry the Vegetables:**

- In the same skillet, add a little more oil if needed.
- Add sliced bell pepper and onion. Stir-fry for about 2-3 minutes until they start to soften.
- Add minced garlic and ginger, and cook for another 30 seconds until fragrant.
- Add snap peas or snow peas and cook for an additional 1-2 minutes.

5. **Combine Everything:**
   - Return the cooked beef to the skillet with the vegetables.
   - Pour the prepared black bean sauce over the beef and vegetables. Stir well to coat everything in the sauce.
   - Bring to a simmer and cook for about 2-3 minutes, allowing the sauce to thicken slightly. If the sauce needs thickening, stir in the cornstarch slurry and cook for an additional minute.

6. **Serve:**
   - Garnish with sliced green onions and fresh cilantro if desired.
   - Serve the Beef with Black Bean Sauce hot over steamed rice.

Enjoy your homemade Beef with Black Bean Sauce, a dish that's both savory and satisfying with its rich, flavorful sauce and tender beef!

Lemon Shrimp

Ingredients:

- **For the Shrimp:**
    - 1 lb (450g) large shrimp, peeled and deveined
    - 2 tablespoons olive oil
    - 3 cloves garlic, minced
    - 1/2 teaspoon red pepper flakes (optional, for heat)
    - Salt and black pepper, to taste
- **For the Lemon Sauce:**
    - Zest and juice of 1 large lemon
    - 1/4 cup chicken or vegetable broth
    - 2 tablespoons butter
    - 1 tablespoon capers (optional, for added flavor)
    - 1 tablespoon chopped fresh parsley (for garnish)
    - Lemon slices (for garnish)

Instructions:

1. **Prepare the Shrimp:**
    - Rinse and pat the shrimp dry with paper towels. Season with salt and black pepper.
2. **Cook the Shrimp:**
    - Heat olive oil in a large skillet over medium-high heat.
    - Add minced garlic and red pepper flakes (if using). Cook for about 30 seconds until fragrant.
    - Add the shrimp to the skillet in a single layer. Cook for 2-3 minutes on each side, or until the shrimp are pink and opaque. Remove the shrimp from the skillet and set aside.
3. **Prepare the Lemon Sauce:**
    - In the same skillet, reduce the heat to medium.
    - Add chicken or vegetable broth and deglaze the pan, scraping up any browned bits from the bottom.
    - Stir in lemon zest, lemon juice, and capers (if using). Bring to a simmer and cook for 1-2 minutes to reduce slightly.
    - Add butter and stir until melted and the sauce is slightly thickened.
4. **Combine and Serve:**
    - Return the cooked shrimp to the skillet and toss to coat in the lemon sauce.
    - Cook for an additional 1-2 minutes until the shrimp are heated through and coated with the sauce.
5. **Garnish and Serve:**
    - Garnish with chopped fresh parsley and lemon slices.
    - Serve hot, over rice, pasta, or alongside a fresh salad.

Enjoy your zesty and delicious Lemon Shrimp, a perfect dish for a quick weeknight meal or a special occasion!

Thai Basil Chicken

Ingredients:

- **For the Stir-Fry:**
    - 1 lb (450g) ground chicken
    - 2 tablespoons vegetable oil
    - 4 cloves garlic, minced
    - 2-4 Thai bird chilies or red chilies, thinly sliced (adjust to your heat preference)
    - 1 small onion, thinly sliced
    - 1 red bell pepper, thinly sliced (optional)
    - 1 cup Thai basil leaves (holy basil is preferred, but regular basil works too)
- **For the Sauce:**
    - 3 tablespoons soy sauce
    - 1 tablespoon fish sauce
    - 1 tablespoon oyster sauce
    - 1 tablespoon sugar
    - 1/4 cup water
- **For Serving:**
    - Cooked jasmine rice
    - Fried eggs (optional, for topping)
    - Extra Thai basil leaves for garnish

Instructions:

1. **Prepare the Sauce:**
    - In a small bowl, mix together soy sauce, fish sauce, oyster sauce, sugar, and water. Stir until the sugar is dissolved. Set aside.
2. **Cook the Chicken:**
    - Heat vegetable oil in a large skillet or wok over medium-high heat.
    - Add minced garlic and sliced chilies. Stir-fry for about 30 seconds until fragrant, being careful not to burn the garlic.
    - Add ground chicken to the skillet. Cook, breaking it up with a spoon, until the chicken is browned and cooked through, about 5-7 minutes.
3. **Add Vegetables:**
    - Add sliced onion and red bell pepper (if using) to the skillet. Stir-fry for 2-3 minutes until the vegetables are tender.
4. **Add the Sauce:**
    - Pour the prepared sauce over the chicken and vegetables. Stir well to coat everything evenly.
    - Cook for an additional 2 minutes, allowing the sauce to heat through and slightly thicken.
5. **Add Basil:**

- - Stir in Thai basil leaves and cook for another minute until the basil is wilted and fragrant.
6. **Serve:**
    - Serve the Thai Basil Chicken hot over jasmine rice.
    - Top with a fried egg if desired, and garnish with extra Thai basil leaves.

Tips:

- **Adjusting Spice Levels:** If you prefer less heat, reduce the number of chilies or remove the seeds.
- **Holy Basil:** If available, use holy basil for a more authentic flavor. Regular basil can be substituted if holy basil is not available.

Enjoy your homemade Thai Basil Chicken, a dish that's both savory and aromatic with a perfect balance of flavors!

Crispy Honey Garlic Chicken

Ingredients:

- **For the Chicken:**
    - 1.5 lbs (680g) boneless, skinless chicken thighs or breasts, cut into bite-sized pieces
    - 1 cup all-purpose flour
    - 1/2 cup cornstarch
    - 1 teaspoon baking powder
    - 1 teaspoon salt
    - 1/2 teaspoon black pepper
    - 1 cup buttermilk (or milk mixed with 1 tablespoon lemon juice)
    - Vegetable oil (for frying)
- **For the Honey Garlic Sauce:**
    - 1/2 cup honey
    - 1/4 cup soy sauce
    - 3 cloves garlic, minced
    - 1 tablespoon minced fresh ginger
    - 1 tablespoon rice vinegar
    - 1 tablespoon cornstarch mixed with 2 tablespoons water (cornstarch slurry)
    - 1 tablespoon sesame oil (optional, for added flavor)
- **For Garnish:**
    - Sesame seeds
    - Chopped green onions
    - Fresh cilantro (optional)

Instructions:

1. **Prepare the Chicken:**
    - In a bowl, combine flour, cornstarch, baking powder, salt, and black pepper.
    - Dip each piece of chicken into the buttermilk, then dredge it in the flour mixture, pressing lightly to coat well.
2. **Fry the Chicken:**
    - Heat vegetable oil in a large skillet or deep fryer to 350°F (175°C). You'll need enough oil to submerge the chicken pieces.
    - Fry the chicken in batches, making sure not to overcrowd the pan. Cook for about 4-6 minutes per batch, or until golden brown and crispy. Remove the chicken and drain on paper towels.
3. **Make the Honey Garlic Sauce:**
    - In a medium saucepan, combine honey, soy sauce, minced garlic, minced ginger, and rice vinegar. Bring to a simmer over medium heat.
    - Stir in the cornstarch slurry and continue to cook for another 1-2 minutes until the sauce thickens.

- Remove from heat and stir in sesame oil if using.
4. **Toss the Chicken in the Sauce:**
   - In a large bowl, toss the crispy chicken pieces with the honey garlic sauce until well coated.
5. **Garnish and Serve:**
   - Transfer the coated chicken to a serving platter.
   - Garnish with sesame seeds, chopped green onions, and fresh cilantro if desired.
   - Serve hot, ideally over steamed rice or with a side of vegetables.

Tips:

- **Crispiness:** For extra crispy chicken, make sure the oil is at the correct temperature and don't overcrowd the pan.
- **Sauce Variations:** Adjust the sweetness or saltiness of the sauce by modifying the amount of honey or soy sauce according to your taste.

Enjoy your Crispy Honey Garlic Chicken with its irresistible combination of crunchy coating and a rich, flavorful sauce!

Sweet and Sour Chicken

Ingredients:

- **For the Chicken:**
    - 1.5 lbs (680g) boneless, skinless chicken breasts or thighs, cut into bite-sized pieces
    - 1 cup all-purpose flour
    - 1/2 cup cornstarch
    - 1 teaspoon baking powder
    - 1 teaspoon salt
    - 1/2 teaspoon black pepper
    - 1 cup buttermilk (or milk mixed with 1 tablespoon lemon juice)
    - Vegetable oil (for frying)
- **For the Sweet and Sour Sauce:**
    - 1/2 cup sugar
    - 1/2 cup rice vinegar
    - 1/4 cup ketchup
    - 1/4 cup soy sauce
    - 1 tablespoon cornstarch mixed with 2 tablespoons water (cornstarch slurry)
    - 1/2 cup water
    - 1 tablespoon vegetable oil
    - 1 clove garlic, minced
    - 1 teaspoon minced fresh ginger
- **For Stir-Frying:**
    - 1 tablespoon vegetable oil
    - 1 bell pepper, cut into chunks (red, green, or a mix)
    - 1 onion, cut into chunks
    - 1 cup pineapple chunks (canned or fresh)
- **For Garnish (optional):**
    - Sesame seeds
    - Chopped green onions

Instructions:

1. **Prepare the Chicken:**
    - In a bowl, mix together flour, cornstarch, baking powder, salt, and black pepper.
    - Dip each piece of chicken into the buttermilk, then dredge it in the flour mixture, pressing lightly to coat well.
2. **Fry the Chicken:**
    - Heat vegetable oil in a large skillet or deep fryer to 350°F (175°C). You'll need enough oil to submerge the chicken pieces.

- Fry the chicken in batches, making sure not to overcrowd the pan. Cook for about 4-6 minutes per batch, or until golden brown and crispy. Remove the chicken and drain on paper towels.

3. **Make the Sweet and Sour Sauce:**
    - In a medium saucepan, heat 1 tablespoon of vegetable oil over medium heat.
    - Add minced garlic and ginger, and cook for about 30 seconds until fragrant.
    - Add sugar, rice vinegar, ketchup, soy sauce, and water. Stir well and bring to a simmer.
    - Stir in the cornstarch slurry and cook for another 1-2 minutes until the sauce thickens. Remove from heat.

4. **Stir-Fry the Vegetables:**
    - In a large skillet or wok, heat 1 tablespoon of vegetable oil over medium-high heat.
    - Add bell peppers and onion, and stir-fry for 2-3 minutes until they start to soften.
    - Add pineapple chunks and cook for another 1-2 minutes.

5. **Combine Everything:**
    - Add the crispy chicken to the skillet with the vegetables and pineapple.
    - Pour the sweet and sour sauce over the chicken and vegetables, and toss to coat everything evenly.
    - Cook for an additional 1-2 minutes to heat through.

6. **Serve:**
    - Transfer the Sweet and Sour Chicken to a serving platter.
    - Garnish with sesame seeds and chopped green onions if desired.
    - Serve hot over steamed rice or noodles.

Tips:

- **Chicken Texture:** For extra crispy chicken, ensure that the oil is hot enough before frying and avoid overcrowding the pan.
- **Sauce Consistency:** Adjust the thickness of the sauce by adding more or less cornstarch slurry as needed.

Enjoy your Sweet and Sour Chicken, a dish that's perfectly balanced with sweet, tangy, and savory flavors!

Dim Sum

Ingredients:

- **For the Filling:**
    - 1/2 pound ground pork
    - 1/2 pound raw shrimp, peeled, deveined, and chopped finely
    - 1/4 cup finely chopped bamboo shoots or water chestnuts (optional, for crunch)
    - 2 tablespoons soy sauce
    - 1 tablespoon oyster sauce
    - 1 teaspoon sesame oil
    - 1 tablespoon cornstarch
    - 1/2 teaspoon sugar
    - 1/2 teaspoon ground white pepper
    - 2 cloves garlic, minced
    - 1 tablespoon ginger, minced
    - 2 green onions, finely chopped
- **For the Dumpling Wrappers:**
    - 20-24 round dumpling wrappers (store-bought or homemade)
- **For Garnish:**
    - Finely chopped carrots or peas (optional, for topping)

Instructions:

1. **Prepare the Filling:**
    - In a large bowl, combine the ground pork, chopped shrimp, bamboo shoots or water chestnuts (if using), soy sauce, oyster sauce, sesame oil, cornstarch, sugar, white pepper, garlic, ginger, and green onions.
    - Mix thoroughly until all ingredients are well combined. You can use your hands or a spoon.
2. **Assemble the Dumplings:**
    - Place a dumpling wrapper in the palm of your hand. Spoon about 1 tablespoon of the filling into the center of the wrapper.
    - Gently pleat the edges of the wrapper around the filling, leaving the top exposed. The dumplings should resemble a little cup or basket.
    - If desired, press a small piece of carrot or a pea on top of each dumpling for garnish.
3. **Steam the Dumplings:**
    - Line a bamboo steamer or a heatproof plate with parchment paper to prevent sticking.
    - Arrange the dumplings in the steamer or on the plate, making sure they don't touch each other.

- Bring water to a boil in a pot or wok, then place the steamer over the boiling water. Cover and steam the dumplings for about 10-12 minutes, or until the filling is cooked through and the wrappers are translucent.
4. **Serve:**
    - Serve the dumplings hot with dipping sauces such as soy sauce, hoisin sauce, or a mixture of soy sauce and rice vinegar.

Enjoy your homemade dim sum!

Shanghai Soup Dumplings

Ingredients:

For the Filling:

- 1/2 pound ground pork (preferably with some fat)
- 1/4 pound shrimp, peeled, deveined, and finely chopped (optional)
- 1/4 cup finely chopped bamboo shoots or water chestnuts (optional)
- 1 tablespoon soy sauce
- 1 tablespoon oyster sauce
- 1 tablespoon rice wine or dry sherry
- 1 teaspoon sesame oil
- 1 tablespoon cornstarch
- 1/2 teaspoon sugar
- 1/2 teaspoon ground white pepper
- 1 tablespoon minced ginger
- 1 tablespoon finely chopped green onions

For the Soup Gelatin:

- 1 cup chicken stock or broth
- 2 teaspoons unflavored gelatin powder

For the Dumpling Dough:

- 2 cups all-purpose flour
- 3/4 cup hot water (more or less, as needed)
- A pinch of salt

Instructions:

1. **Prepare the Soup Gelatin:**
    - Heat the chicken stock in a small saucepan until warm. Sprinkle the gelatin powder over the surface and let it sit for a few minutes to bloom.
    - Stir until the gelatin is fully dissolved. Pour the mixture into a shallow dish and refrigerate until set, about 1-2 hours. Once set, cut the gelatin into small cubes.
2. **Prepare the Filling:**
    - In a large bowl, combine the ground pork, chopped shrimp (if using), bamboo shoots or water chestnuts (if using), soy sauce, oyster sauce, rice wine, sesame oil, cornstarch, sugar, white pepper, ginger, and green onions. Mix well.
    - Gently fold in the gelatin cubes until evenly distributed.
3. **Make the Dough:**
    - In a large bowl, mix the flour and salt. Gradually add the hot water, stirring continuously until a dough forms.

- Knead the dough on a lightly floured surface until smooth, about 5-7 minutes. Cover with a damp cloth and let it rest for at least 30 minutes.

4. **Assemble the Dumplings:**
   - Divide the dough into small pieces (about 20-24). Roll each piece into a thin circle, about 3-4 inches in diameter.
   - Place a spoonful of filling in the center of each wrapper. Carefully pleat the edges of the dough around the filling, pinching and twisting to seal the top. Make sure the dumplings are well-sealed to prevent leaks.

5. **Steam the Dumplings:**
   - Line a bamboo steamer with parchment paper or lightly grease it to prevent sticking. Arrange the dumplings in the steamer, making sure they are not touching each other.
   - Bring a pot of water to a boil, then place the steamer over the boiling water. Cover and steam the dumplings for about 12-15 minutes, or until the filling is cooked through and the wrappers are translucent.

6. **Serve:**
   - Serve the soup dumplings hot with dipping sauces like soy sauce, rice vinegar, and thinly sliced ginger.

Enjoy your delicious homemade Xiao Long Bao!

Hot Pot

Ingredients:

For the Broth:

- 6 cups chicken or vegetable stock
- 2-3 slices ginger
- 2-3 cloves garlic, smashed
- 2-3 scallions, cut into large pieces
- 2-3 dried chilies (optional, for spice)
- 2-3 star anise (optional, for aroma)
- 2 tablespoons soy sauce
- 1 tablespoon rice wine or dry sherry
- 1 tablespoon miso paste or salt (to taste)

For the Dipping Sauces:

- Soy sauce
- Sesame oil
- Rice vinegar
- Hoisin sauce
- Chili paste (for heat)
- Fresh herbs (like cilantro, mint) and minced garlic (optional)

For the Hot Pot Ingredients:

- Thinly sliced meats (beef, pork, lamb)
- Seafood (shrimp, fish fillets, mussels)
- Fresh vegetables (bok choy, mushrooms, spinach, napa cabbage)
- Tofu (firm or silken, cut into cubes)
- Noodles (udon, rice noodles, or glass noodles)
- Dumplings or meatballs (optional)

Instructions:

1. **Prepare the Broth:**
    - In a large pot, combine the chicken or vegetable stock with ginger, garlic, scallions, dried chilies, star anise, soy sauce, rice wine, and miso paste.
    - Bring to a boil, then reduce heat and let it simmer for about 15-20 minutes to allow the flavors to meld. Strain out the solids if desired, and keep the broth hot.
2. **Prepare the Dipping Sauces:**
    - Set up a dipping sauce station with soy sauce, sesame oil, rice vinegar, hoisin sauce, and chili paste. Feel free to mix and match according to your taste. You can also add chopped fresh herbs and minced garlic for extra flavor.

3. **Prepare the Hot Pot Ingredients:**
    - Arrange the sliced meats, seafood, vegetables, tofu, noodles, and any additional items on large platters.
    - If using frozen dumplings or meatballs, thaw them before serving.
4. **Set Up the Hot Pot:**
    - Transfer the hot broth to a portable burner or hot pot appliance on the dining table. Keep it simmering throughout the meal.
    - Provide chopsticks or tongs for cooking and serving the ingredients.
5. **Cook and Enjoy:**
    - Each person can add their chosen ingredients to the simmering broth, cooking them to their preferred doneness. Thinly sliced meats and seafood cook quickly, while vegetables and tofu take a bit longer.
    - Once cooked, transfer the ingredients to your bowl, dip them into your favorite dipping sauces, and enjoy.
6. **Refill and Repeat:**
    - Refill the pot with additional broth or water as needed, and continue cooking and enjoying until everyone is satisfied.

Hot Pot is highly customizable and can be adapted to suit your tastes and dietary preferences. It's a great way to enjoy a variety of flavors and ingredients in a single, communal meal. Enjoy your Hot Pot experience!

Teriyaki Chicken

Ingredients:

For the Chicken:

- 4 boneless, skinless chicken thighs or breasts
- 1 tablespoon vegetable oil
- Salt and pepper to taste

For the Teriyaki Sauce:

- 1/2 cup soy sauce
- 1/4 cup mirin (sweet rice wine) or dry sherry
- 1/4 cup sake (Japanese rice wine) or white wine
- 1/4 cup brown sugar or honey
- 2 tablespoons rice vinegar
- 2 cloves garlic, minced
- 1 teaspoon fresh ginger, minced or grated
- 1 tablespoon cornstarch mixed with 1 tablespoon water (for thickening, optional)
- Sesame seeds and chopped green onions for garnish (optional)

Instructions:

1. **Prepare the Teriyaki Sauce:**
    - In a saucepan, combine the soy sauce, mirin, sake, brown sugar, rice vinegar, garlic, and ginger.
    - Bring the mixture to a boil over medium heat, stirring to dissolve the sugar.
    - Reduce the heat and simmer for 5-7 minutes until slightly thickened. If you prefer a thicker sauce, stir in the cornstarch mixture and cook for an additional 1-2 minutes until the sauce has thickened to your liking. Remove from heat and set aside.
2. **Prepare the Chicken:**
    - Season the chicken with salt and pepper.
    - Heat the vegetable oil in a large skillet over medium-high heat.
    - Add the chicken to the skillet and cook for 5-7 minutes per side, or until the chicken is cooked through and has a nice golden-brown color. The internal temperature should reach 165°F (75°C).
3. **Glaze the Chicken:**
    - Once the chicken is cooked, reduce the heat to medium and pour half of the teriyaki sauce over the chicken.
    - Cook for an additional 2-3 minutes, turning the chicken to coat it evenly with the sauce and allow it to caramelize slightly.
4. **Serve:**

- Slice the chicken into strips or bite-sized pieces.
- Drizzle the remaining teriyaki sauce over the chicken or serve it on the side for dipping.
- Garnish with sesame seeds and chopped green onions, if desired.

5. **Accompaniments:**
    - Serve the Teriyaki Chicken with steamed rice, sautéed vegetables, or a fresh salad for a complete meal.

This recipe gives you a delicious Teriyaki Chicken with a perfect balance of sweet and savory flavors. Enjoy your homemade Teriyaki Chicken!

Shrimp with Lobster Sauce

Ingredients:

For the Shrimp:

- 1 pound large shrimp, peeled and deveined
- 1 tablespoon vegetable oil
- 2 cloves garlic, minced
- 1 teaspoon fresh ginger, minced

For the Lobster Sauce:

- 1 cup chicken or seafood stock
- 1 tablespoon soy sauce
- 1 tablespoon oyster sauce
- 1 tablespoon rice wine or dry sherry
- 1 teaspoon sugar
- 1 tablespoon cornstarch mixed with 2 tablespoons water (for thickening)
- 2 tablespoons fermented black beans, rinsed and mashed (optional, for added depth)
- 1 egg, beaten
- 1/4 cup frozen peas (optional)
- Salt and pepper to taste
- 2 green onions, chopped (for garnish)

Instructions:

1. **Prepare the Shrimp:**
    - Heat the vegetable oil in a large skillet or wok over medium-high heat.
    - Add the minced garlic and ginger, and sauté for about 30 seconds until fragrant.
    - Add the shrimp to the skillet and cook for 2-3 minutes on each side, or until they turn pink and are cooked through. Remove the shrimp from the skillet and set aside.
2. **Make the Lobster Sauce:**
    - In the same skillet, add the chicken or seafood stock, soy sauce, oyster sauce, rice wine, and sugar. Stir well and bring to a simmer.
    - If using fermented black beans, add them to the sauce and stir.
    - Slowly stir in the cornstarch mixture to thicken the sauce. Cook for 1-2 minutes until the sauce has thickened to your liking.
    - Reduce the heat to low and slowly pour in the beaten egg, stirring gently to create egg ribbons in the sauce.
    - If using frozen peas, add them to the sauce and cook for another 1-2 minutes until they are heated through.
    - Season the sauce with salt and pepper to taste.

3. **Combine and Serve:**
    - Return the cooked shrimp to the skillet and toss them in the sauce to coat evenly. Cook for an additional 1-2 minutes to heat the shrimp through and meld the flavors.
    - Garnish with chopped green onions.
4. **Serve:**
    - Serve the Shrimp with Lobster Sauce over steamed rice or with a side of vegetables.

Enjoy your homemade Shrimp with Lobster Sauce! This dish is flavorful and perfect for a quick weeknight dinner or a special occasion.

Chinese BBQ Ribs

Ingredients:

For the Marinade:

- 1/2 cup hoisin sauce
- 1/4 cup soy sauce
- 1/4 cup honey or maltose
- 2 tablespoons Chinese rice wine or dry sherry
- 2 tablespoons sugar (brown sugar or white sugar)
- 1 tablespoon sesame oil
- 2 cloves garlic, minced
- 1 tablespoon fresh ginger, minced
- 1 teaspoon five-spice powder
- 1 teaspoon red food coloring (optional, for traditional red color)
- 1/4 teaspoon white pepper

For the Ribs:

- 2 pounds pork ribs (baby back or spare ribs)
- 1 tablespoon vegetable oil (for roasting)

Instructions:

1. **Prepare the Marinade:**
    - In a bowl, combine the hoisin sauce, soy sauce, honey, rice wine, sugar, sesame oil, garlic, ginger, five-spice powder, red food coloring (if using), and white pepper. Mix well.
2. **Marinate the Ribs:**
    - Pat the ribs dry with paper towels. Remove any excess fat and silver skin from the ribs if necessary.
    - Place the ribs in a large resealable plastic bag or a shallow dish. Pour half of the marinade over the ribs, making sure they are well-coated. Reserve the remaining marinade for basting.
    - Seal the bag or cover the dish and refrigerate for at least 4 hours, or overnight for the best flavor.
3. **Preheat the Oven:**
    - Preheat your oven to 300°F (150°C).
4. **Prepare for Roasting:**
    - Line a baking sheet with aluminum foil and place a wire rack on top. Brush the rack with vegetable oil to prevent sticking.
    - Remove the ribs from the marinade and place them on the wire rack. Discard any leftover marinade that has touched the raw meat.

5. **Roast the Ribs:**
   - Roast the ribs in the preheated oven for about 2.5 to 3 hours, or until the meat is tender and easily pulls away from the bone.
   - Baste the ribs with the reserved marinade every 30 minutes during the roasting process to build up a nice glaze. If you want a more caramelized finish, you can also brush with honey during the last 15-20 minutes of roasting.
6. **Broil for a Finish (Optional):**
   - If you prefer a more charred exterior, switch the oven to broil and broil the ribs for an additional 3-5 minutes, watching carefully to avoid burning.
7. **Serve:**
   - Remove the ribs from the oven and let them rest for a few minutes before slicing between the bones.
   - Serve the ribs with steamed rice, stir-fried vegetables, or a side of pickled vegetables.

Enjoy your delicious homemade Chinese BBQ Ribs! They're perfect for a special meal or a tasty treat any time.

Prawn and Chive Dumplings

Ingredients:

For the Filling:

- 1/2 pound (225g) raw prawns, peeled and deveined
- 1/2 cup fresh chives, finely chopped
- 1 tablespoon ginger, minced
- 1 tablespoon soy sauce
- 1 tablespoon oyster sauce
- 1 teaspoon sesame oil
- 1 tablespoon cornstarch
- 1/2 teaspoon sugar
- 1/4 teaspoon white pepper

For the Dumpling Wrappers:

- 20-24 round dumpling wrappers (store-bought or homemade)

For Steaming:

- Bamboo steamer or a heatproof plate lined with parchment paper

Instructions:

1. **Prepare the Filling:**
   - Chop the prawns into small pieces. You can use a knife or pulse them briefly in a food processor until finely chopped but not pureed.
   - In a bowl, combine the chopped prawns, chives, minced ginger, soy sauce, oyster sauce, sesame oil, cornstarch, sugar, and white pepper. Mix well until the ingredients are thoroughly combined.
2. **Assemble the Dumplings:**
   - Place a dumpling wrapper on a clean surface. Spoon about 1 tablespoon of filling into the center of the wrapper.
   - Wet the edges of the wrapper with a little water using your finger or a brush. Fold the wrapper in half to create a half-moon shape, pinching the edges to seal. You can also pleat the edges for a traditional look if desired.
   - Repeat with the remaining wrappers and filling.
3. **Prepare for Steaming:**
   - Line a bamboo steamer with parchment paper or lightly grease it to prevent sticking. Arrange the dumplings in the steamer, making sure they don't touch each other.
   - If using a heatproof plate, place the dumplings on it, lined with parchment paper.
4. **Steam the Dumplings:**

- Bring a pot of water to a boil. Place the bamboo steamer or heatproof plate over the boiling water, making sure it doesn't touch the water.
- Cover and steam the dumplings for about 10-12 minutes, or until the wrappers are translucent and the filling is cooked through.

5. **Serve:**
    - Serve the dumplings hot with dipping sauces such as soy sauce, vinegar, or a combination of soy sauce and sesame oil. You can also serve them with a side of chili sauce for extra flavor.

These prawn and chive dumplings are a delicious and satisfying addition to any dim sum spread or as a standalone treat. Enjoy your homemade dumplings!

Salt and Pepper Squid

Ingredients:

For the Squid:

- 1 pound (450g) fresh squid, cleaned and sliced into rings or strips
- 1/2 cup all-purpose flour
- 1/4 cup cornstarch
- 1 teaspoon baking powder
- 1/2 teaspoon salt
- 1/2 teaspoon black pepper
- 1/2 teaspoon white pepper (optional)
- 1/2 teaspoon Chinese five-spice powder (optional)
- 1/2 teaspoon garlic powder (optional)

For Frying:

- Vegetable oil (for deep-frying)

For Garnish:

- 2-3 cloves garlic, thinly sliced
- 2-3 fresh red or green chilies, sliced (or dried chili flakes)
- 2-3 sprigs fresh cilantro, chopped (optional)
- Lemon wedges (optional)

Instructions:

1. **Prepare the Squid:**
    - Clean the squid by removing the head, innards, and cartilage. Rinse well and pat dry with paper towels.
    - Slice the squid into rings or strips, depending on your preference.
2. **Prepare the Coating:**
    - In a large bowl, combine the flour, cornstarch, baking powder, salt, black pepper, white pepper (if using), Chinese five-spice powder (if using), and garlic powder (if using).
    - Toss the squid pieces in the flour mixture until evenly coated. You can also put the squid and flour mixture in a resealable plastic bag and shake to coat.
3. **Heat the Oil:**
    - Heat about 2-3 inches of vegetable oil in a deep skillet or wok over medium-high heat. To check if the oil is ready, drop a small piece of the coating mixture into the oil; it should sizzle and rise to the surface.
4. **Fry the Squid:**

- Working in batches, carefully add the coated squid pieces to the hot oil. Fry for about 2-3 minutes, or until golden brown and crispy. Avoid overcrowding the pan to ensure even frying.
- Use a slotted spoon to remove the squid from the oil and drain on a plate lined with paper towels.

5. **Prepare the Garnish:**
   - In a separate small pan, heat a little oil over medium heat. Add the garlic slices and sliced chilies (or chili flakes) and cook until the garlic is golden brown and crispy, about 1-2 minutes. Be careful not to burn the garlic.

6. **Serve:**
   - Arrange the fried squid on a serving platter. Sprinkle with the crispy garlic and chili mixture. Garnish with chopped cilantro if desired.
   - Serve immediately with lemon wedges on the side, if using.

Tips:

- **For Tender Squid:** Be sure not to overcook the squid, as it can become tough and rubbery. Fry in small batches to keep the oil temperature consistent.
- **For Extra Crunch:** You can double-coat the squid by dipping it in the flour mixture, then in a beaten egg, and then back in the flour mixture before frying.

Enjoy your crispy, flavorful Salt and Pepper Squid! It's perfect as an appetizer or a tasty snack.

Chinese Broccoli with Oyster Sauce

Ingredients:

- 1 bunch Chinese broccoli (Gai Lan), washed and trimmed
- 2 tablespoons vegetable oil
- 2 cloves garlic, minced
- 2 tablespoons oyster sauce
- 1 tablespoon soy sauce
- 1 tablespoon water
- 1 teaspoon sugar
- 1/2 teaspoon sesame oil (optional, for added flavor)
- Cooked rice or noodles (optional, for serving)

Instructions:

1. **Prepare the Chinese Broccoli:**
   - Trim the tough ends of the Chinese broccoli stems. If the stems are very thick, you can slice them in half lengthwise to ensure they cook evenly.
   - Blanch the Chinese broccoli in boiling water for about 2-3 minutes until the stems are tender but still crisp. The leaves should be wilted. Drain and immediately plunge the broccoli into a bowl of ice water to stop the cooking process. Drain again and set aside.
2. **Make the Sauce:**
   - In a small bowl, mix together the oyster sauce, soy sauce, water, and sugar. Stir until the sugar is dissolved. Set aside.
3. **Stir-Fry the Garlic:**
   - Heat the vegetable oil in a large skillet or wok over medium heat.
   - Add the minced garlic and cook for about 30 seconds, or until fragrant but not browned.
4. **Add the Broccoli:**
   - Add the blanched Chinese broccoli to the skillet with the garlic. Stir-fry for about 1-2 minutes to heat through and combine with the garlic.
5. **Add the Sauce:**
   - Pour the prepared sauce over the broccoli and toss to coat evenly. Cook for another 1-2 minutes, allowing the sauce to heat through and slightly thicken.
6. **Finish and Serve:**
   - Drizzle with sesame oil if using, and toss to combine.
   - Transfer to a serving plate and serve immediately, either on its own or alongside rice or noodles.

Tips:

- **Blanching:** Blanching the Chinese broccoli helps to preserve its vibrant green color and ensures it remains tender-crisp.
- **Customize the Sauce:** You can adjust the amount of sugar or soy sauce according to your taste preferences. For a touch of heat, consider adding a pinch of chili flakes or a dash of hot sauce.
- **Presentation:** For a more refined presentation, arrange the Chinese broccoli neatly on the plate and drizzle the sauce over it.

This dish is a fantastic addition to any Chinese meal, offering a balance of flavors and a pleasing texture. Enjoy your Chinese Broccoli with Oyster Sauce!

Beef Chow Fun

Ingredients:

For the Marinade:

- 8 oz (225g) beef flank steak or sirloin, thinly sliced
- 1 tablespoon soy sauce
- 1 tablespoon oyster sauce
- 1 tablespoon rice wine or dry sherry
- 1 teaspoon cornstarch
- 1/2 teaspoon sugar
- 1/2 teaspoon sesame oil

For the Stir-Fry:

- 8 oz (225g) wide rice noodles (fresh or dried, preferably)
- 2 tablespoons vegetable oil
- 2 cloves garlic, minced
- 1 tablespoon ginger, minced
- 1 onion, sliced
- 1 bell pepper, sliced
- 2-3 green onions, chopped
- 1 cup bean sprouts
- 2 tablespoons soy sauce
- 1 tablespoon oyster sauce
- 1 tablespoon dark soy sauce (for color, optional)
- 1 teaspoon sugar
- 1/2 teaspoon white pepper
- 1 teaspoon sesame oil (optional, for added flavor)

Instructions:

1. **Prepare the Noodles:**
   - **If using dried rice noodles:** Cook according to package instructions until just tender. Drain and rinse under cold water to stop cooking. Toss with a little vegetable oil to prevent sticking.
   - **If using fresh rice noodles:** Separate the noodles and set aside.
2. **Marinate the Beef:**
   - In a bowl, combine the sliced beef with soy sauce, oyster sauce, rice wine, cornstarch, sugar, and sesame oil. Mix well and let it marinate for about 15-20 minutes.
3. **Stir-Fry the Beef:**
   - Heat 1 tablespoon of vegetable oil in a large skillet or wok over high heat.

- Add the marinated beef and stir-fry for 2-3 minutes until browned and cooked through. Remove the beef from the skillet and set aside.

4. **Stir-Fry the Vegetables:**
   - In the same skillet or wok, add the remaining tablespoon of vegetable oil.
   - Add the minced garlic and ginger, and stir-fry for about 30 seconds until fragrant.
   - Add the sliced onion and bell pepper, and stir-fry for another 2 minutes until they start to soften.

5. **Combine and Finish:**
   - Add the cooked noodles and bean sprouts to the skillet with the vegetables. Stir-fry for 1-2 minutes to combine.
   - Return the cooked beef to the skillet. Add soy sauce, oyster sauce, dark soy sauce (if using), sugar, and white pepper. Stir everything together and cook for another 2-3 minutes until everything is heated through and well coated with the sauce.
   - Drizzle with sesame oil if using, and toss to combine.

6. **Serve:**
   - Garnish with chopped green onions.
   - Serve hot as a main dish or alongside other Chinese dishes.

Tips:

- **Beef:** For the best texture, slice the beef thinly against the grain. Marinating the beef helps tenderize it and adds flavor.
- **Noodles:** If using fresh rice noodles, you may need to separate them gently with your hands if they're sticking together.
- **High Heat:** Stir-fry on high heat to achieve that characteristic "wok hei" (breath of the wok) flavor and a slightly smoky aroma.

Enjoy your homemade Beef Chow Fun! It's a flavorful, satisfying dish that's perfect for a quick weeknight dinner or a special meal.

Egg Foo Young

Ingredients:

For the Egg Foo Young:

- 4 large eggs
- 1/2 cup cooked chicken, pork, or shrimp (diced, optional)
- 1/2 cup bean sprouts
- 1/4 cup mushrooms, sliced (shiitake or button mushrooms work well)
- 1/4 cup green onions, chopped
- 1/4 cup carrots, finely diced
- 2 tablespoons soy sauce
- 1 tablespoon oyster sauce (optional)
- 1/2 teaspoon sesame oil
- Salt and pepper to taste
- 2 tablespoons vegetable oil (for frying)

For the Brown Sauce:

- 1 cup chicken or vegetable broth
- 2 tablespoons soy sauce
- 1 tablespoon oyster sauce
- 1 tablespoon cornstarch mixed with 2 tablespoons water (for thickening)
- 1 teaspoon sugar
- 1/2 teaspoon white pepper
- 1/2 teaspoon sesame oil (optional)

Instructions:

1. **Prepare the Egg Mixture:**
    - In a large bowl, beat the eggs until well mixed. Add the soy sauce, oyster sauce (if using), sesame oil, salt, and pepper. Mix well.
    - Gently fold in the diced meat (if using), bean sprouts, mushrooms, green onions, and carrots.
2. **Cook the Egg Foo Young:**
    - Heat 1 tablespoon of vegetable oil in a non-stick skillet or wok over medium heat.
    - Pour about 1/4 of the egg mixture into the skillet, spreading it out to form a pancake.
    - Cook for 2-3 minutes until the edges are set and the bottom is golden brown. Flip the pancake and cook the other side for another 1-2 minutes until cooked through. Transfer to a plate and keep warm.
    - Repeat with the remaining egg mixture, adding more oil to the skillet as needed.
3. **Prepare the Brown Sauce:**

- In a small saucepan, combine the chicken or vegetable broth, soy sauce, oyster sauce, sugar, and white pepper. Bring to a boil over medium heat.
- Stir in the cornstarch mixture and cook, stirring constantly, until the sauce thickens, about 1-2 minutes.
- Remove from heat and stir in sesame oil if using.

4. **Serve:**
    - Pour the brown sauce over the Egg Foo Young or serve it on the side for dipping.
    - Serve hot with steamed rice or noodles.

Tips:

- **Ingredients:** Feel free to customize the filling ingredients based on what you have on hand. Bell peppers, snow peas, or water chestnuts are great additions.
- **Texture:** For fluffier omelets, beat the eggs thoroughly and ensure the skillet is well-oiled and preheated.
- **Thickening Sauce:** Adjust the cornstarch mixture for a thicker or thinner sauce to your preference.

Egg Foo Young is versatile and can be adapted to suit different tastes and dietary preferences. Enjoy this classic Chinese-American dish!

Crab Fried Rice

Ingredients:

- 2 cups cooked jasmine or long-grain rice (preferably cold and a day old for better texture)
- 8 oz (225g) fresh crab meat (or canned crab meat, drained and picked over for shells)
- 2 tablespoons vegetable oil
- 2 cloves garlic, minced
- 1 small onion, finely chopped
- 1/2 cup bell pepper, diced (red or green)
- 1/2 cup carrots, diced
- 2 green onions, chopped
- 2 large eggs, lightly beaten
- 2 tablespoons soy sauce
- 1 tablespoon oyster sauce
- 1 teaspoon sesame oil
- Salt and pepper to taste
- Optional: 1/2 cup frozen peas or corn (thawed)
- Optional garnish: chopped cilantro or additional green onions

Instructions:

1. **Prepare the Ingredients:**
   - If using leftover rice, break up any clumps. Ensure the rice is cold for best results.
   - Pick through the crab meat to remove any shell fragments.
2. **Cook the Vegetables:**
   - Heat 1 tablespoon of vegetable oil in a large skillet or wok over medium-high heat.
   - Add the minced garlic and chopped onion, and stir-fry for about 1 minute until fragrant.
   - Add the diced bell pepper and carrots (and peas or corn if using) to the skillet. Stir-fry for about 2-3 minutes until the vegetables are tender.
3. **Scramble the Eggs:**
   - Push the vegetables to one side of the skillet.
   - Add the remaining 1 tablespoon of vegetable oil to the empty side of the skillet.
   - Pour in the beaten eggs and scramble until cooked through. Combine with the vegetables.
4. **Add the Rice:**
   - Add the cold rice to the skillet. Use a spatula to break up any remaining clumps and mix the rice with the vegetables and eggs.
   - Stir-fry for about 3-4 minutes until the rice is heated through and well combined with the vegetables.
5. **Season the Rice:**

- Add the crab meat to the skillet and gently fold it into the rice. Be careful not to break up the crab meat too much.
- Stir in the soy sauce, oyster sauce, and sesame oil. Mix well to evenly coat the rice.
- Season with salt and pepper to taste. Adjust the seasoning if needed.

6. **Garnish and Serve:**
   - Stir in the chopped green onions and cook for another minute.
   - Garnish with additional green onions or chopped cilantro if desired.
   - Serve hot, either on its own or as a side dish with other Chinese or Asian-inspired dishes.

Tips:

- **Rice:** Using cold, day-old rice helps to achieve the best texture for fried rice. Freshly cooked rice can become mushy.
- **Crab Meat:** If using fresh crab, you can steam and pick the meat yourself. Canned crab meat is a convenient alternative.
- **Customization:** Feel free to add other ingredients like mushrooms, bell peppers, or even a splash of rice vinegar for extra flavor.

Enjoy your homemade Crab Fried Rice—it's a perfect way to enjoy the delicate flavor of crab in a hearty and satisfying dish!

Cantonese Roast Pork

Ingredients:

For the Marinade:

- 2 pounds (900g) pork shoulder or pork belly, cut into 1-inch thick strips
- 1/4 cup hoisin sauce
- 1/4 cup soy sauce
- 1/4 cup honey or maltose
- 2 tablespoons Chinese rice wine or dry sherry
- 2 tablespoons sugar (brown or white)
- 1 tablespoon oyster sauce
- 1 tablespoon sesame oil
- 2 cloves garlic, minced
- 1 tablespoon fresh ginger, minced
- 1 teaspoon five-spice powder
- 1 teaspoon red food coloring (optional, for traditional color)

For Glazing and Roasting:

- 2 tablespoons honey mixed with 1 tablespoon warm water (for glazing)
- 1 tablespoon soy sauce (for glazing)

Instructions:

1. **Prepare the Marinade:**
   - In a bowl, mix together the hoisin sauce, soy sauce, honey, rice wine, sugar, oyster sauce, sesame oil, garlic, ginger, five-spice powder, and red food coloring (if using).
2. **Marinate the Pork:**
   - Place the pork strips in a large resealable plastic bag or a shallow dish.
   - Pour the marinade over the pork, making sure the meat is evenly coated.
   - Seal the bag or cover the dish and refrigerate for at least 4 hours, or preferably overnight for the best flavor.
3. **Preheat the Oven:**
   - Preheat your oven to 375°F (190°C).
4. **Prepare for Roasting:**
   - Line a baking sheet with aluminum foil and place a wire rack on top. Brush the rack with vegetable oil to prevent sticking.
   - Remove the pork from the marinade and place it on the wire rack. Reserve the marinade for basting.
5. **Roast the Pork:**
   - Roast the pork in the preheated oven for about 30 minutes.

- After 30 minutes, brush the pork with a mixture of honey and water. This will give the pork a glossy finish.
- Continue roasting for another 20-30 minutes, or until the pork is caramelized and cooked through. You may need to turn the pork halfway through the cooking time for even coloring.
- If desired, broil the pork for an additional 3-5 minutes at the end to achieve a more charred exterior, watching carefully to avoid burning.

6. **Glaze and Finish:**
   - During the last 10 minutes of roasting, brush the pork with a mixture of soy sauce and honey for added flavor and color.
   - Once done, remove the pork from the oven and let it rest for 5-10 minutes before slicing.

7. **Serve:**
   - Slice the Char Siu into thin pieces.
   - Serve with steamed rice, noodles, or use it in other dishes such as fried rice or bao buns.

Tips:

- **Marination Time:** For the best flavor, marinate the pork overnight.
- **Pork Cut:** Pork shoulder or pork belly works best for this recipe due to its balance of meat and fat, which keeps it juicy and flavorful.
- **Glazing:** Multiple layers of glazing help achieve a deep, caramelized color and enhance the flavor.

Enjoy your homemade Cantonese Roast Pork! It's a flavorful dish that's perfect for a hearty meal or for adding to other recipes.

Sichuan Cold Noodles

Ingredients:

For the Noodles:

- 8 oz (225g) Chinese egg noodles or thin wheat noodles (can substitute with other noodles of your choice)
- 1/2 cucumber, julienned
- 1/2 carrot, julienned
- 2-3 green onions, finely chopped
- 1/4 cup fresh cilantro, chopped (optional)

For the Sauce:

- 3 tablespoons sesame paste (or tahini if you can't find sesame paste)
- 2 tablespoons soy sauce
- 2 tablespoons rice vinegar
- 1 tablespoon Chinese black vinegar (optional, for deeper flavor)
- 2 tablespoons chili oil (adjust to taste)
- 1 tablespoon sugar
- 1 teaspoon Sichuan peppercorns, toasted and ground (or 1/2 teaspoon ground black pepper as a substitute)
- 1 clove garlic, minced
- 1 tablespoon ginger, minced
- 1 tablespoon hoisin sauce (optional, for added sweetness)
- 1 tablespoon sesame oil

Instructions:

1. **Prepare the Noodles:**
    - Cook the noodles according to package instructions until al dente.
    - Drain and rinse under cold water to cool them down and remove excess starch. Toss with a little vegetable oil to prevent sticking.
2. **Make the Sauce:**
    - In a bowl, combine the sesame paste, soy sauce, rice vinegar, black vinegar (if using), chili oil, sugar, ground Sichuan peppercorns, garlic, ginger, and hoisin sauce (if using).
    - Whisk until the mixture is smooth and well combined. Adjust the seasoning to taste. If the sauce is too thick, you can thin it with a bit of water or additional rice vinegar.
3. **Assemble the Dish:**
    - In a large mixing bowl, toss the cooked and cooled noodles with the sauce until evenly coated.

- Add the julienned cucumber, carrot, and chopped green onions. Toss gently to combine.
4. **Serve:**
   - Transfer the noodles to serving plates or bowls.
   - Garnish with fresh cilantro if desired.

Tips:

- **Sichuan Peppercorns:** These add a unique numbing spiciness that's characteristic of Sichuan cuisine. If you can't find them, ground black pepper is a good substitute, though the flavor will be slightly different.
- **Chili Oil:** Adjust the amount of chili oil based on your heat preference. You can also add a sprinkle of chili flakes if you like extra spice.
- **Make Ahead:** This dish can be prepared in advance and kept in the refrigerator for a few hours or overnight. The flavors will meld together as it sits.

Enjoy your Sichuan Cold Noodles as a refreshing, spicy, and flavorful dish that's perfect for any occasion!

Black Pepper Beef

Ingredients:

For the Beef Marinade:

- 1 pound (450g) beef sirloin or flank steak, thinly sliced against the grain
- 1 tablespoon soy sauce
- 1 tablespoon rice wine or dry sherry
- 1 teaspoon cornstarch
- 1/2 teaspoon sugar
- 1/2 teaspoon sesame oil

For the Stir-Fry:

- 2 tablespoons vegetable oil
- 2 cloves garlic, minced
- 1 tablespoon fresh ginger, minced
- 1 onion, sliced
- 1 bell pepper, sliced (any color)
- 1 cup mushrooms, sliced (shiitake or button mushrooms work well)
- 2 tablespoons soy sauce
- 1 tablespoon oyster sauce
- 2 tablespoons black pepper (adjust to taste)
- 1/2 cup beef broth or water
- 1 teaspoon cornstarch mixed with 1 tablespoon water (for thickening)
- Optional: 1 tablespoon hoisin sauce (for added sweetness)
- Cooked rice for serving

Instructions:

1. **Marinate the Beef:**
    - In a bowl, combine the sliced beef with soy sauce, rice wine, cornstarch, sugar, and sesame oil. Mix well and let it marinate for at least 15-20 minutes.
2. **Prepare the Stir-Fry:**
    - Heat 1 tablespoon of vegetable oil in a large skillet or wok over medium-high heat.
    - Add the marinated beef in a single layer and cook for about 2-3 minutes on each side until browned but not fully cooked. Remove the beef from the skillet and set aside.
3. **Cook the Vegetables:**
    - In the same skillet, add the remaining tablespoon of vegetable oil.
    - Add the minced garlic and ginger, and stir-fry for about 30 seconds until fragrant.

- Add the sliced onion, bell pepper, and mushrooms. Stir-fry for about 3-4 minutes until the vegetables are tender-crisp.
4. **Combine and Finish:**
    - Return the partially cooked beef to the skillet with the vegetables.
    - Add soy sauce, oyster sauce, and black pepper. Stir well to combine.
    - Pour in the beef broth or water and bring to a simmer. Cook for an additional 2-3 minutes, allowing the flavors to meld and the sauce to slightly reduce.
    - Stir in the cornstarch mixture to thicken the sauce. Cook for another minute or until the sauce has reached your desired consistency.
    - If using, add the hoisin sauce for a touch of sweetness.
5. **Serve:**
    - Serve the Black Pepper Beef hot over steamed rice.

Tips:

- **Beef Cut:** Thinly sliced beef helps ensure quick cooking and tender texture. Sirloin or flank steak are good choices for this dish.
- **Pepper Level:** Adjust the amount of black pepper to your taste. For a milder flavor, use less pepper, and for a spicier kick, increase the amount.
- **Cornstarch:** If you prefer a thicker sauce, you can add a bit more cornstarch mixture. Just be sure to cook it long enough to remove any raw cornstarch taste.

Enjoy your homemade Black Pepper Beef—it's a flavorful, satisfying dish that's perfect for a quick weeknight dinner or a special meal!

Chinese Chicken Salad

Ingredients:

For the Salad:

- 2 cups cooked chicken breast, shredded or diced (you can use leftover chicken or rotisserie chicken)
- 4 cups mixed salad greens (such as Romaine, iceberg, and/or spinach)
- 1 cup shredded cabbage (green or purple)
- 1/2 cup shredded carrots
- 1/2 cup sliced bell pepper (any color)
- 1/2 cup sliced cucumber
- 1/4 cup thinly sliced green onions
- 1/4 cup chopped fresh cilantro (optional)
- 1/4 cup toasted almonds or cashews (optional, for crunch)
- 1/4 cup crispy chow mein noodles or fried wonton strips (optional, for additional crunch)

For the Dressing:

- 1/4 cup rice vinegar
- 3 tablespoons soy sauce
- 2 tablespoons sesame oil
- 2 tablespoons honey or sugar
- 1 tablespoon hoisin sauce (optional, for extra depth of flavor)
- 1 teaspoon freshly grated ginger
- 1 clove garlic, minced
- 1 tablespoon water (to adjust consistency, if needed)

Instructions:

1. **Prepare the Chicken:**
   - If not already cooked, poach or grill the chicken breasts until fully cooked. Let them cool, then shred or dice into bite-sized pieces.
2. **Prepare the Vegetables:**
   - Wash and chop the salad greens, shred the cabbage and carrots, and slice the bell pepper and cucumber.
   - Place all the vegetables in a large mixing bowl.
3. **Make the Dressing:**
   - In a small bowl or jar, whisk together the rice vinegar, soy sauce, sesame oil, honey, hoisin sauce (if using), grated ginger, and minced garlic.
   - Taste and adjust the seasoning if needed. If the dressing is too thick, add a tablespoon of water to reach your desired consistency.
4. **Assemble the Salad:**

- Add the shredded chicken to the bowl of vegetables.
- Pour the dressing over the salad and toss well to coat all ingredients evenly.
5. **Garnish and Serve:**
    - Garnish with chopped cilantro, toasted almonds or cashews, and crispy chow mein noodles or fried wonton strips if using.
    - Serve immediately or chill in the refrigerator for up to an hour before serving.

Tips:

- **Chicken:** Using rotisserie chicken or leftover chicken makes this recipe quick and convenient. For a lighter option, use grilled or poached chicken breast.
- **Crunchy Toppings:** The crispy chow mein noodles or wonton strips add a delightful crunch. Add them just before serving to keep them crisp.
- **Adjusting Flavor:** Feel free to adjust the sweetness or tanginess of the dressing to suit your taste. If you prefer a spicier kick, add a touch of chili paste or red pepper flakes.

Enjoy your Chinese Chicken Salad—a perfect blend of textures and flavors that's both satisfying and refreshing!

Tofu and Vegetable Stir-Fry

Ingredients:

For the Tofu:

- 14 oz (400g) firm tofu, drained and pressed
- 2 tablespoons soy sauce
- 1 tablespoon cornstarch
- 2 tablespoons vegetable oil (for frying)

For the Stir-Fry:

- 2 tablespoons vegetable oil
- 2 cloves garlic, minced
- 1 tablespoon fresh ginger, minced
- 1 bell pepper, sliced (any color)
- 1 cup broccoli florets
- 1 carrot, sliced thinly
- 1 cup snap peas or snow peas
- 1/2 cup sliced mushrooms (shiitake, button, or cremini)
- 2 green onions, chopped
- 2 tablespoons soy sauce
- 1 tablespoon oyster sauce or hoisin sauce (optional)
- 1 tablespoon rice vinegar
- 1 teaspoon sesame oil
- 1 tablespoon water or vegetable broth (for thinning the sauce if needed)

For Garnish (optional):

- Sesame seeds
- Chopped cilantro or basil
- Additional sliced green onions

Instructions:

1. **Prepare the Tofu:**
   - Cut the pressed tofu into bite-sized cubes.
   - Toss the tofu cubes with soy sauce and cornstarch until evenly coated.
2. **Cook the Tofu:**
   - Heat 2 tablespoons of vegetable oil in a large non-stick skillet or wok over medium-high heat.
   - Add the tofu cubes and cook until golden brown and crispy on all sides, about 5-7 minutes. Remove the tofu from the skillet and set aside.
3. **Stir-Fry the Vegetables:**

- In the same skillet, add 2 tablespoons of vegetable oil.
- Add the minced garlic and ginger, and stir-fry for about 30 seconds until fragrant.
- Add the bell pepper, broccoli, carrot, snap peas, and mushrooms. Stir-fry for 4-5 minutes, or until the vegetables are tender-crisp.

4. **Add the Tofu and Sauce:**
   - Return the cooked tofu to the skillet with the vegetables.
   - In a small bowl, mix together soy sauce, oyster sauce or hoisin sauce (if using), rice vinegar, and sesame oil.
   - Pour the sauce over the tofu and vegetables. Stir well to combine and cook for an additional 2-3 minutes until everything is heated through and the sauce is slightly thickened. If the sauce is too thick, add a tablespoon of water or vegetable broth to reach your desired consistency.

5. **Garnish and Serve:**
   - Garnish with sesame seeds, chopped cilantro or basil, and additional sliced green onions if desired.
   - Serve hot over steamed rice, noodles, or enjoy as a stand-alone dish.

Tips:

- **Pressing Tofu:** Pressing the tofu helps to remove excess moisture, which makes it crisp up better when frying. You can use a tofu press or wrap the tofu in a clean kitchen towel and place a heavy object on top for about 15 minutes.
- **Vegetables:** Feel free to customize the vegetables based on what you have on hand. Bell peppers, carrots, broccoli, and snap peas are just a few suggestions.
- **Sauce Variations:** Adjust the sauce ingredients according to your taste. For more heat, add a splash of chili sauce or red pepper flakes.

This **Tofu and Vegetable Stir-Fry** is a balanced, flavorful dish that's both satisfying and adaptable to different tastes and dietary needs. Enjoy your meal!

Honey Walnut Shrimp

Ingredients:

For the Walnuts:

- 1 cup walnut halves
- 1/2 cup sugar
- 1/2 cup water

For the Shrimp:

- 1 pound (450g) large shrimp, peeled and deveined
- 1/2 cup cornstarch
- 1/2 cup all-purpose flour
- 1/2 teaspoon salt
- 1/4 teaspoon black pepper
- 1 large egg, beaten
- Vegetable oil (for frying)

For the Sauce:

- 1/4 cup mayonnaise
- 1/4 cup honey
- 1 tablespoon lemon juice
- 1 tablespoon sweetened condensed milk (optional, for extra creaminess)

Instructions:

1. **Prepare the Walnuts:**
    - In a small saucepan, combine the sugar and water. Bring to a simmer over medium heat, stirring until the sugar is dissolved.
    - Add the walnut halves to the saucepan. Simmer for about 3-4 minutes, allowing the walnuts to absorb the syrup.
    - Remove the walnuts from the syrup using a slotted spoon and place them on a baking sheet lined with parchment paper. Let them cool and harden, which should take about 10-15 minutes.
2. **Prepare the Shrimp:**
    - In a bowl, mix the cornstarch, flour, salt, and pepper.
    - Dredge each shrimp in the flour mixture, shaking off the excess.
    - Dip the coated shrimp into the beaten egg, then coat again in the flour mixture.
3. **Fry the Shrimp:**
    - Heat about 2 inches of vegetable oil in a large skillet or wok over medium-high heat (to about 350°F or 175°C).

- Fry the shrimp in batches, without overcrowding the pan, until golden and crispy, about 2-3 minutes per side. Remove the shrimp with a slotted spoon and drain on paper towels.
4. **Prepare the Sauce:**
     - In a medium bowl, mix together the mayonnaise, honey, lemon juice, and sweetened condensed milk (if using). Stir until smooth and well combined.
5. **Combine and Serve:**
     - Toss the crispy shrimp with the honey sauce until well coated.
     - Gently fold in the cooled, candied walnuts.
     - Serve immediately, garnished with extra walnuts if desired.

Tips:

- **Walnut Texture:** Ensure the walnuts are fully coated with the syrup and cooled completely to achieve the right crunchiness.
- **Frying Shrimp:** For best results, maintain the oil temperature and fry the shrimp in small batches to ensure they stay crispy.
- **Sauce Variation:** Adjust the sweetness of the sauce by varying the amount of honey or condensed milk to your taste.

This **Honey Walnut Shrimp** recipe offers a delightful combination of sweet, creamy, and crunchy elements, making it a standout dish for any meal or special occasion. Enjoy!

Szechuan Eggplant

Ingredients:

For the Eggplant:

- 2 large eggplants (Chinese or Japanese eggplants preferred, but regular eggplant works too)
- 2 tablespoons vegetable oil (for frying)
- 1 tablespoon soy sauce
- 1 tablespoon rice vinegar
- 1 tablespoon sugar
- 1 teaspoon cornstarch mixed with 1 tablespoon water (for thickening)

For the Sauce:

- 2 tablespoons vegetable oil
- 3 cloves garlic, minced
- 1 tablespoon fresh ginger, minced
- 2 tablespoons doubanjiang (Szechuan bean paste) or chili paste
- 2 tablespoons soy sauce
- 1 tablespoon rice vinegar
- 1 tablespoon hoisin sauce (optional, for added sweetness)
- 1 tablespoon sugar (adjust to taste)
- 1/2 cup vegetable broth or water
- 1 teaspoon toasted sesame oil
- 1 teaspoon Szechuan peppercorns, toasted and ground (optional, for authentic flavor)
- 2 green onions, chopped (for garnish)
- Sesame seeds (for garnish)

Instructions:

1. **Prepare the Eggplant:**
    - Cut the eggplants into bite-sized pieces or slices.
    - Heat 2 tablespoons of vegetable oil in a large skillet or wok over medium-high heat.
    - Add the eggplant pieces in batches (don't overcrowd the pan) and cook until golden brown and tender, about 5-7 minutes per batch. Remove the cooked eggplant and set aside on paper towels to drain excess oil.
2. **Prepare the Sauce:**
    - In the same skillet, add 2 tablespoons of vegetable oil.
    - Add the minced garlic and ginger, and stir-fry for about 30 seconds until fragrant.
    - Add the doubanjiang (or chili paste) and stir-fry for another 30 seconds to release its flavors.

3. **Combine the Ingredients:**
    - Return the cooked eggplant to the skillet.
    - Add soy sauce, rice vinegar, hoisin sauce (if using), sugar, and vegetable broth or water.
    - Stir well to coat the eggplant with the sauce.
    - Bring to a simmer and cook for 2-3 minutes, allowing the sauce to reduce slightly and thicken.
    - Stir in the cornstarch mixture to thicken the sauce further. Cook for an additional 1-2 minutes until the sauce has thickened to your liking.
4. **Finish and Serve:**
    - Stir in the toasted sesame oil and ground Szechuan peppercorns (if using).
    - Garnish with chopped green onions and sesame seeds.
    - Serve hot with steamed rice or as part of a larger meal.

Tips:

- **Eggplant Texture:** For a firmer texture, you can also roast the eggplant pieces in the oven instead of frying them.
- **Doubanjiang:** This Szechuan bean paste adds authentic flavor and heat. Adjust the amount based on your spice tolerance.
- **Adjusting Spice Level:** You can control the spiciness by adding more or less doubanjiang or chili paste.

Enjoy your **Szechuan Eggplant**—a flavorful, spicy dish that's perfect for adding some excitement to your meals!

Steamed Fish with Ginger and Scallions

Ingredients:

- 1 whole fish (about 1.5 to 2 pounds), such as sea bass, tilapia, or snapper, cleaned and scaled
- 2-3 slices fresh ginger
- 3-4 scallions, cut into 3-inch lengths
- 2 tablespoons soy sauce
- 1 tablespoon rice wine or dry sherry
- 1 tablespoon sesame oil
- 1 tablespoon vegetable oil
- 1/2 teaspoon salt
- Fresh cilantro (optional, for garnish)

Instructions:

1. **Prepare the Fish:**
   - Rinse the fish under cold water and pat it dry with paper towels.
   - Make a few diagonal cuts on each side of the fish to help it cook evenly and absorb flavors.
2. **Season the Fish:**
   - Rub the fish inside and out with salt.
   - Place a few slices of ginger and scallion lengths inside the cavity of the fish.
3. **Prepare the Steaming Setup:**
   - Place a heatproof plate that fits inside your steamer or a large skillet with a lid.
   - Arrange a few additional ginger slices and scallion pieces on top of the fish. This adds flavor and helps to infuse the fish during steaming.
4. **Steam the Fish:**
   - Fill the steamer or skillet with about 2 inches of water and bring to a boil.
   - Place the plate with the fish into the steamer or on a rack above the boiling water. If using a skillet, place the plate on a steaming rack or a small dish that keeps it elevated above the water.
   - Cover and steam for 8-12 minutes, depending on the thickness of the fish. The fish is done when it flakes easily with a fork.
5. **Prepare the Sauce:**
   - While the fish is steaming, heat the vegetable oil in a small saucepan until hot.
   - Combine the soy sauce, rice wine, and sesame oil in a small bowl.
   - Once the fish is done, carefully remove it from the steamer or skillet.
   - Discard the ginger and scallions on top of the fish.
6. **Finish the Dish:**
   - Pour the soy sauce mixture evenly over the steamed fish.
   - Drizzle the hot vegetable oil over the fish. The hot oil will sizzle and enhance the flavors.

- Garnish with fresh cilantro if desired.
7. **Serve:**
    - Serve the fish immediately with steamed rice.

Tips:

- **Fish Selection:** Fresh fish works best for this recipe. Ensure the fish has clear eyes, bright red gills, and a fresh smell.
- **Steaming Time:** Adjust the steaming time based on the size and thickness of the fish. If you're unsure, check the fish a minute or two earlier to avoid overcooking.
- **Flavor Variations:** You can add thinly sliced mushrooms, a small amount of soy sauce, or a splash of vinegar to the steaming liquid for additional flavor.

This **Steamed Fish with Ginger and Scallions** is a simple yet elegant dish that brings out the natural flavors of the fish while adding aromatic and savory notes. Enjoy this healthy and flavorful meal!

Chinese Scallion Pancakes

Ingredients:

For the Dough:

- 2 cups all-purpose flour
- 3/4 cup boiling water
- 1/4 cup cold water
- 1/2 teaspoon salt
- 2 tablespoons vegetable oil (for dough)

For the Filling:

- 1/2 cup scallions, finely chopped
- 1/4 cup vegetable oil (for brushing and frying)
- 1/2 teaspoon salt
- 1/2 teaspoon sesame oil (optional, for added flavor)

Instructions:

1. **Prepare the Dough:**
   - In a large bowl, mix the flour and salt.
   - Gradually add the boiling water, stirring with a fork or chopsticks until a shaggy dough forms.
   - Add the cold water and mix until the dough comes together. If too dry, add a bit more water.
   - Knead the dough on a floured surface for about 5-7 minutes until smooth. Cover with a damp cloth and let it rest for at least 30 minutes.
2. **Prepare the Filling:**
   - In a small bowl, combine the chopped scallions, salt, and sesame oil if using.
3. **Roll Out the Dough:**
   - Divide the dough into 4 equal pieces.
   - On a floured surface, roll out one piece of dough into a thin rectangle or circle, about 1/8-inch thick.
4. **Add the Filling:**
   - Brush a thin layer of vegetable oil over the rolled-out dough.
   - Evenly sprinkle a quarter of the scallion mixture over the dough.
5. **Shape the Pancake:**
   - Roll the dough up tightly into a log or cylinder.
   - Coil the dough into a spiral shape, tucking the ends underneath to form a round shape.
   - Gently flatten the coiled dough with your hand, then roll out again into a flat pancake about 1/4-inch thick.

6. **Cook the Pancakes:**
   - Heat 2 tablespoons of vegetable oil in a skillet over medium heat.
   - Cook the pancake for 2-3 minutes per side, or until golden brown and crispy. Adjust heat as necessary to prevent burning.
   - Remove from the skillet and drain on paper towels. Repeat with the remaining dough.
7. **Serve:**
   - Cut the pancakes into wedges and serve warm with soy sauce or a dipping sauce of your choice.

Tips:

- **Dough Consistency:** The dough should be smooth and pliable. If it's too sticky, add a bit more flour; if too dry, add a little more water.
- **Rolling Out:** Roll out the dough as thin as possible to get more layers and a crispier texture.
- **Oil:** Use a generous amount of oil when cooking to achieve a crispy exterior.

Enjoy your **Chinese Scallion Pancakes**—crispy, savory, and perfect for any occasion!

Lotus Leaf Wrapped Chicken

Ingredients:

For the Marinade:

- 1 whole chicken (about 2 to 3 pounds), cut into bite-sized pieces (or 4 chicken thighs/breasts, cut into pieces)
- 2 tablespoons soy sauce
- 1 tablespoon oyster sauce
- 1 tablespoon rice wine or dry sherry
- 1 tablespoon hoisin sauce
- 1 tablespoon sugar
- 1 teaspoon sesame oil
- 1 teaspoon five-spice powder
- 1/2 teaspoon white pepper
- 1 tablespoon cornstarch

For the Filling:

- 1/2 cup dried shiitake mushrooms, soaked and sliced
- 1/2 cup water chestnuts, diced
- 1/2 cup bamboo shoots, sliced
- 2-3 dried lotus leaves (available at Asian grocery stores)

For Garnish (optional):

- Chopped cilantro or green onions
- Steamed rice

Instructions:

1. **Prepare the Lotus Leaves:**
    - Rinse the dried lotus leaves under cold water to remove any dirt.
    - Soak the lotus leaves in warm water for about 30 minutes, or until they become pliable. Drain and pat dry.
2. **Marinate the Chicken:**
    - In a large bowl, combine the soy sauce, oyster sauce, rice wine, hoisin sauce, sugar, sesame oil, five-spice powder, white pepper, and cornstarch.
    - Add the chicken pieces and toss well to coat. Let it marinate for at least 30 minutes, or up to 2 hours in the refrigerator for more flavor.
3. **Prepare the Filling:**
    - If using dried shiitake mushrooms, soak them in warm water until softened, then slice.
    - Combine the mushrooms, water chestnuts, and bamboo shoots in a bowl.

4. **Wrap the Chicken:**
    - Cut each lotus leaf into large squares, enough to wrap the chicken pieces.
    - Place a few pieces of the marinated chicken in the center of each leaf.
    - Top with some of the mushroom, water chestnut, and bamboo shoot mixture.
    - Fold the lotus leaf over the chicken, tucking the edges underneath to form a neat package. Secure with kitchen twine if necessary.
5. **Steam the Chicken:**
    - Prepare a steamer or large pot with a steaming rack. If using a pot, add water to the bottom of the pot and bring to a boil.
    - Arrange the wrapped chicken packets on the steaming rack, making sure they don't touch each other.
    - Steam over medium-high heat for about 30-40 minutes, or until the chicken is cooked through and tender.
6. **Serve:**
    - Carefully unwrap the lotus leaves and transfer the chicken to a serving platter.
    - Garnish with chopped cilantro or green onions if desired.
    - Serve hot with steamed rice.

Tips:

- **Lotus Leaves:** If you can't find lotus leaves, you can use parchment paper as an alternative, though it won't impart the same aroma.
- **Marinating Time:** The longer you marinate the chicken, the more flavorful it will be. However, even a short marination will still be delicious.
- **Steaming:** Ensure the steaming water does not touch the chicken packets to avoid sogginess.

This **Lotus Leaf Wrapped Chicken** is a delightful and aromatic dish that brings a taste of traditional Chinese cooking to your table. Enjoy the unique flavors and tender texture of this special recipe!

www.ingramcontent.com/pod-product-compliance
Lightning Source LLC
LaVergne TN
LVHW081601060526
838201LV00054B/2006